Discipline: Positive Attitudes for Learning

Foundations of Secondary Education
Jean D. Grambs, Editor

Discipline: Positive Attitudes for Learning

MICHAEL H. JESSUP and MARGARET A. KILEY
Towson State College

Prentice-Hall, Inc., Englewood Cliffs, New Jersey

Jean Grambs, consulting editor

© 1971 by Prentice-Hall, Inc., Englewood Cliffs, New Jersey

C: 13–215863–9
P: 13–215855–8

Library of Congress Catalog Card Number: 71–149356

Current printing (last digit):
10   9   8   7   6   5   4   3   2   1

Printed in the United States of America

        Prentice-Hall International, Inc., London
        Prentice-Hall of Australia, Pty. Ltd., Sydney
        Prentice-Hall of Canada, Ltd., Toronto
        Prentice-Hall of India Private Limited, New Delhi
        Prentice-Hall of Japan, Inc., Tokyo

TO
Joanne
Michael
Mark

Foreword

Whenever we admiringly comment that someone is a "born teacher," implicit in our observation is the assumption that this person is able to help young people learn in an atmosphere of serenity and good humor. Since so few individuals are "born teachers" we must provide ways for prospective teachers to develop the insights and skills that seem to come so naturally to these favored few.

Some of the things "good" teachers *do* elude the untrained observer. "His classes are so orderly, how does he do it?" is the perplexed comment of the teacher-to-be. Some of what the good teacher does comes from experience: knowing some of the probable responses youth will make to differing expectations, activities, seasons. But for the truly good teacher, who seems as effective on blue Monday as on frantic Friday, with moody Alice or insolent Larry, there is more than just good instincts at work. These good teachers are sensitive observers, flexible in their own responses, with a repertoire of behaviors which match and meet the infinite variety of personalities in their classrooms.

The good teacher represents the application of good theory. The literature of education is overflowing with critical dissections of today's secondary schools. Unfortunately, prescriptions for remedying the observed failures tend only too often to wander off into the wild blue yonder, remote from the reality of the school. The search for "practical" ways of turning good theory into good practice has produced a shelf full of discipline guides. The volume that Professors Jessup and Kiley have written is based on a careful review of what has already been done, plus their own years of experience in teacher education. So far we have not found *the* book which can give the new teacher some of the savvy and experience of the "born teacher." Hopefully, this volume marks distinct progress toward that goal.

The authors have sought out good theory, translated this into typical school and classroom situations, and finally, into specific incidents. The bridge between general principles and specific applications is spelled out sensitively and judiciously. As the authors well know, individual teaching style evolves from the personality each individual brings into the teaching situation; there are no formulas that, if applied, guarantee the right answer every time. The book therefore has the unique inclusion of do-it-yourself case material. The reader along with his classmates can not only suggest solutions *in practice* that seem to make sense to him, to fit his own view of appropriate behavior, but also he can discuss his version with others. He will then see something he may have missed, the blind spots induced by limited experience or a particular kind of personality, and therefore benefits from the whole range of life styles and value systems which are to be found in a college classroom.

If we believe that our secondary school classrooms should be —must be—student-centered, then in fact we must also make our college classrooms similar. It is only as the student learns that he can change his behavior. This volume, then, is student-centered. It puts the learning task upon the reader, and in turn, provides a setting where he can learn with and from his peers and his instructors.

We are on the verge of exciting new developments in secondary school curriculum and school organization. In fact, the school must change—or perish. But change can only occur where teachers and students feel at ease with each other. This is good discipline. And this is what we feel will be the contribution of this volume to the education of teachers.

JEAN DRESDEN GRAMBS
University of Maryland

Preface

During years of teaching and then observing student teachers in rural, urban, and suburban secondary schools, we have become convinced that classroom control is an overriding concern of both new and experienced teachers.

What has happened? Has the very nature of secondary school teaching changed so drastically over the past few years? Or is it possible that our teachers are no longer able to maintain the proper climate for learning in the classroom because of changes in the world of youth and therefore must spend their time controlling instead of teaching? Perhaps this is what teachers now face.

In a nationwide poll,[1] parents of secondary school students named disciplining their children to conform as one of the most important functions of the school. In past years the establishment of correct behavioral patterns was considered a parental and school responsibility to be accomplished before the child reached secondary school age.

The increased problem of classroom control may well stem from the fact that today's teacher has be-

[1]Louis Harris, "The Life Poll," *Life*, 66, No. 19 (May 16, 1969): 29.

come a parent surrogate and suddenly finds he is asked to assume duties that he feels ill-equipped to handle. He discovers that in his changing role he may be acting more like a policeman than a teacher. Yet a teacher must develop the appropriate climate in his classroom before he can begin to do any teaching.

For some teachers maintaining an atmosphere conducive to teaching and learning is *not* a problem. They thoroughly enjoy their classroom experiences with the challenging and inquisitive young minds placed in their charge. At the same time, however, other teachers find themselves locked in a struggle with their students (ironically these are frequently the same students the other teachers label a "joy" to teach!). What makes the difference in the behavior of students from one class to another? Could it be the difference in the behavior of various teachers or the subject or the time of day?

We have taken the position that good teaching and discipline are the same in all secondary schools—rural, urban, and suburban. The difference is in the dimension of the problems which occur. Our approach has been not to dwell on any one particular area but to draw anecdotes and classroom situations from various types of secondary schools.

We wish to express our appreciation to Dr. Jean D. Grambs for her assistance, direction, and encouragement. Special recognition is due Joanne L. Jessup for typing the manuscript and "pushing" the authors when they tended to fall behind in their work.

MICHAEL H. JESSUP
MARGARET A. KILEY

Contents

xi

Discipline: Positive Attitudes for Learning

Introduction

Like little Red Riding Hood scampering merrily along to her adventure at grandmother's house, the inexperienced teacher arrives at the classroom door filled with enthusiasm, eager to impart the world's knowledge to his young charges. We all know what almost happened to that heroine, and in this book, we shall attempt to illustrate what *might* happen to an equally unwary teacher.

We will probe the causes of student behavior and misbehavior and offer some ideas for establishing good classroom atmosphere and thereby decreasing the probability of future discipline problems.

Teacher preparation programs need to give more effective attention to the entire area of classroom control. Therefore, this book should prove especially useful for those preparing to enter the exciting, rewarding, but sometimes frustrating, world of the teacher. Experienced teachers will find our approach helpful since this book takes the position that reactions to classroom situations arising from deviant behavior are understandable and can be readily dealt with. While reflecting upon their own experiences in the classroom and visualizing the situations illustrated, teachers will find it obvious that many so-called discipline problems stem from events which in reality are quite trivial, often ridiculous, and sometimes pathetic. Undue emphasis on such problems wastes valuable class time and can lead to deeper student alienation.

There is no one tried-and-true, never-fail solution to the problems that may occur, though beginning teachers wish there were. We believe that developing a flexible, "open" approach to the handling of student problems will help provide the key to establishing and maintaining a successful learning climate in the classroom. Administrators concerned with the growing problems of effective classroom control can also utilize the principles and situations in this book for discussion at teacher workshops and in-service seminars.

This book is not meant to be a replacement for any textbook dealing with the broad field of secondary education. Rather, it is a much-needed supplement. The treatment of discipline in general texts is necessarily rather brief and thus of little practical assistance to the teacher who needs specifics.

Our hypothesis, as exemplified by the situations included in some of the chapters, is that there are several ways of handling any problem which occurs in the classroom. Because all teachers and students are unique individuals, what works for one teacher may fail for another. The personality of the teacher, the rapport he enjoys with his class, the temperament of the student causing the problem at that particular moment will combine to influence the course of action which the teacher chooses. That is, the teacher must act upon one of the options available to him at that time. We have termed this choice an *Action Option*.

Plan of the Book

The book is divided into six chapters. Chapter One will provide a setting for the entire book. After a brief treatment of the nature of discipline, the importance of providing the proper climate for an effective teaching-learning situation is explored in some detail. And the proposition that the personal philosophy of the teacher will affect his reactions to each classroom situation is examined.

Problems that occur in the classroom result from a breakdown in communications and in human relationships that often arises from events which, in actuality, were trivial. The improvement of human relations requires both self-understanding and the realization of the effects of one's own personality on others.

Chapters Two through Five deal with classroom problems that originate with the teacher, student, administrator, and parent respectively. Any one of these various members of the school community may, through their choice of a specific action option, precipitate a classroom problem or crisis.

Throughout the first five chapters certain principles or hypotheses will be presented. At the end of Chapters Two, Three, Four, and Five, situations are presented together with action options to illustrate the points being covered. These will supply the reader with material for detailed analysis and discussion.

The final chapter will present our conclusions.

Using the Situations

Each of the situations presented may be used in a variety of ways. The reader may analyze the material independently focusing on several aspects of the situation: (1) With which of the individuals is he sympathetic? (2) Has he identified with any particular individual? (3) Has he formed any positive or negative reactions to the individuals involved? Of course, the question to be answered is *why* does the reader feel as he does. Projecting himself into the various roles presented in the situation could provide a clearer perception of the behaviors illustrated, thus enabling the reader to understand more fully his own reactions.

After an initial analysis, the reader may try to seek causes for the described behavior and select an action option for the problem presented. Blame may even be affixed to one of the characters in the situation. More than one reading could cause the reader to reevaluate his initial impressions and question his original premises. Notes made during the first reading, when reexamined, could also prove useful in analyzing the reasons for the original choice of action option.

The greatest effectiveness, however, will result when the situations are used within a class where a variety of opinions are presented and several action options discussed. If there are enough students, the class could be divided into groups of no more than five members. Each group would work independently to arrive at a tentative solution. These findings could then be discussed by the entire class. The rationale for arriving at these varying conclusions, as well as the logic and differing philosophies of the participants should prove enlightening. Through the discussion of the various action options selected, it will become evident that each individual may perceive the same set of circumstances somewhat differently from the other members of his group or any other group. Such differences of opinion do *not* mean that one individual must be right and the others wrong.

Role-Playing and Video-Taping

If facilities are available for group study, the participants could role play these situations using tape or videotape. A more thorough analysis will be achieved after a playback of the tape. By stopping the tape at selected points, the group participants could be questioned about their emotions as they played their special roles. They then could be asked to recall exactly what they felt and what they meant to convey at any precise moment, and why they responded as they did. The other members of the class could then share their individual reactions to the behavior they had observed. They would thus be provided an opportunity to examine the differences in what they *assumed* the participant meant by the exhibited behavior and what the participant now *says* he felt and meant by his actions.

Thus the participants and the entire class would have the opportunity to explore their own feeling when standing in the shoes of an assumed character in the role-playing situation. The participants should gain a clearer insight into how their actions are evaluated and interpreted by others—perhaps even seeing ourselves, as Robert Burns expressed it, as others see us.

1

Setting

"Don't those girls ever stop talking?"

"Why can't he sit still?"

"He's the most sullen kid in school, a born troublemaker."

"I can't stand that stupid grin on her face!"

"Why can't they understand that cheating only hurts themselves?"

"If he talks back to me one more time. I'm going to flunk him."

Introduction

From these samples of "teacher-talk," it would appear that, to adults, the adolescent is a complex creature indeed. He has changed considerably over the past few years from a seemingly passive, obedient child, bowing to the many wishes and demands of his various teachers, into a more critically thinking individual. His inclination now is not to say "yes" to any direction without first thinking or asking "why?" Not only does he want to know the reason he is expected to learn certain material or act in a certain manner, but he expects the reasons given to be valid in terms of his present needs and expectations. Because of this stress on the

5

"now" of things, he is very present-oriented. Teacher responses such as "Learning _____ will help to make you a well-rounded individual," or "The knowledge gained in _____ will help you in the future," are considered by students poor justification for the study of any subject. They want to learn, but they feel many of their studies are unrelated to the world in which they live.

The various media—radio, motion pictures, magazines, books, newspapers, and especially television—have provided them with knowledge denied to past generations. Students are able to see, hear, and read about events as they are happening. What is more important, they form their *own* opinions concerning these events.

A student leader today has watched various college campuses erupt with violence over student dissatisfaction with the institutions' course offerings or instructional attitudes. These demonstrations provided him with proof that when students unite under a common banner, they can become a force powerful enough to make the "establishment" quake in its boots and bring about the desired changes. Many of the youth of today feel they understand the issues and problems of concern to them: war, peace, poverty, racial injustice, and the depersonalization of society. These are *their* problems and they are anxious to begin working toward solutions, but they feel hemmed in by arbitrary school rules forcing their attention elsewhere.

Although there have been encouraging efforts by some schools to update their curriculum and improve their teaching strategies, unfortunately too many secondary classrooms have remained on the fringes of what is happening in real life. A curriculum designed solely to preserve the existing culture and traditions of the past can be maddening to a present-oriented adolescent.

The student is forced to turn off his real-life interests when he enters the classroom and, in turn, substitute his artificial school interests. Some are able to make this transition more easily than others. For those students who view their junior and senior high school years as progressing toward entrance into college, the shift in behavior is accomplished through the necessity of complying with the system. But for the youth who envisions the secondary school as probably being his final connection with formalized education, the dichotomy between real life and school life is often too wide to accept comfortably or complacently.

It is into this structure and amidst these feelings that the secondary teacher moves. Frequently his goals for the educative process come into direct conflict with those of his students. Teachers see school and their particular subject matter from a far different perspective than do their students.

When an individual decides that teaching is going to be his career—his way of life—he usually explains his desire to teach in terms of reaching young people, stimulating young minds, opening new vistas. No dark clouds cross his bright horizon, no doubts enter his mind that the students entrusted to him may have any reluctance about going down the golden path in search of truth and wisdom. Not until he is about to begin his student teaching does he finally permit himself to wonder whether *every* student is, in fact, an eager learner. Doubts quickly become fears and these prospective teachers begin to seek desperately some magic elixir to guarantee effective classroom order or control.

Classroom Control (What is it?)   Classroom control is that technique or method which the teacher develops within the framework of existing school rules to provide the proper learning climate for his students. It is a very individual matter. Each teacher must decide for himself those conditions under which he can function and his students learn most effectively. For some teachers, a quiet classroom symbolizes the educative process. Others encourage student interaction and accept the ensuing noise as being an integral part of the learning process.

Need for Guidelines (Help, Anyone!)   Yet in spite of the individual nature of classroom control, every new teacher seeks some form of guidance. This is quite understandable. Classroom control is probably the largest single cause of teacher and student frustration.

Even experienced teachers often find classroom control the most onerous part of the teaching process. The entire procedure would be greatly simplified if control could be divided into lists of specific "Do's and Don't's" which could be committed to memory and then used as needed. However, the achievement of an effective climate for learning often goes beyond a simple listing of mechanical tasks into more complex areas. At the same time, there are some general tenets concerning control which can be discussed and upon which agreement can be reached.

Students bring into each classroom a wide range of problems from outside sources, from their homes, peer groups, and from other classes. None of these problems may be directly related to the particular teacher or class in which the student is seated at that moment. Yet if they remain uppermost in the student's mind, or if they are unintentionally aggravated by the teacher's actions, an open problem may develop within the classroom. Therefore, although these concerns may be considered abstract since they are not of the teacher's making, they definitely deserve his concern.

Other problems, however, which develop in class may be directly related to the teacher and his relationship with the class. They can be classified as being of a more simple nature since they can be more quickly controlled by the teacher. In fact, some are apparently so simple that they are often ignored as being too trivial to matter. But if anything which distracts the student from the learning process is considered important, then there is no such thing as an insignificant classroom problem.

Teachers

Some individuals choose to teach because they have a deep interest in history, mathematics, music, languages, sports, or science. They may visualize themselves in the role of master scholar, artist, or athlete dispensing wisdom to a spellbound audience. Many have little understanding of and less affection for the adolescents they are to teach.

In discussing teaching with college students, one of the authors is continually amazed (and appalled!) that prospective teachers seem totally unable to answer the question, "Why do you want to be a teacher?" When pressed, the reply is usually, "Well, because I like history" (or whatever the subject may be). It comes as quite a nasty shock to some of these future teachers when they realize that they must teach their beloved subject to teenage students. After the first days of student teaching, they also see that these students do not sit docilely in their seats, pencils poised, eager to take copious notes. Instead, they giggle, squirm, talk out loud, and could care less how or why Hannibal got those elephants over the Alps or that a triangle has three sides.

After four years behind the protection of ivy-covered college walls, the secondary school can be somewhat terrifying to an individual who fails to see that teaching is more than talking, fact giving, and report writing. A teacher must give of himself; he must reach out to his students, making them aware of him not only as a teacher but as an adult concerned about them as individuals. To do this, he must not only like his subject matter (and be competent in it) but he must be willing to expend great amounts of energy, every day, to communicate his knowledge to his students.

The young lady who enters teaching because "it's a nice, respectable job for the few years ahead before marriage" (and her retirement from the work force) ; the boy hoping to stay draft exempt ("I'd rather face those grubby 7th graders than live ammo") ; those who just don't know what to do after graduation ("after all, you only work 190 days a year and the pay's not bad") will find the demands of teaching excessive. Hopefully, they will soon become discouraged from continuing in a profession to which they are unwilling or unable to make a total commitment.

The individual who will succeed in the classroom is one with an integrated personality, who has chosen his professional career carefully, aware of its problems as well as its rewards. He certainly likes his subject, but he also likes young people and wants to share with them the excitement of learning. His self-image is sufficiently secure and well-defined that incidents occurring in the classroom will not be magnified out of proportion. Misbehavior is not interpreted as a personal affront but is handled with calm, deliberate action.

Perhaps we should pause a moment and consider some of the components of a secure self-image. What enables an individual to accept himself, confident to undertake responsibilities, able to relate successfully to others? Those who would instruct and guide impressionable adolescents should certainly be mature adults who have come to grips with the questions of "Who am I?," "Why am I here?," and "Where am I going?" Obviously, complete answers to these queries usually take the better part of a lifetime, but the secure individual feels he is at least on the right path in finding his answers.

Developing an integrated and acceptable sense of self[1] requires the creation of an internal environment in which the individual feels others regard him as a person of worth, despite shortcomings and failures. Furthermore, he feels that his opinions, suggestions, and contributions are welcomed and will be listened to with respect. He achieves success more often than he experiences failure. Consequently, he is unafraid to reveal his feelings to others, even to students, and thus he encourages their self-expression. Yet, because teachers are human, and, therefore, less than perfect, they are not always successful in providing an atmosphere of self-acceptance.

It should be remembered that teachers bring into the classroom

[1]For a comprehensive treatment of the development of the concept of self, see Carl R. Rogers, *On Becoming a Person* (Boston: Houghton Mifflin Company, 1961).

their own values and prejudices, conscious and unconscious. Some may find themselves in a school serving a student population whose culture differs from their own and where the norm of acceptable behavior varies greatly from what they have known.

Prior to their student teaching experience, many prospective teachers have not developed a philosophy regarding classroom control. As student teachers, they saw what "worked" for other teachers and may have adopted some techniques without asking themselves "Why do I think this was a good way to handle that problem?" or "What was the effect on the student and on the teacher's rapport with his students?" or "What motivated the teacher to use this tactic?" Perhaps unconsciously the new teacher acquires a pattern of responses to student behavior, responses which if examined critically would prove inappropriate.

Very often when teachers attempt to understand why they are not as effective in their teaching as they had hoped to be, or why the class is not attentive or interested in the material under consideration, they usually omit the most obvious factor—themselves.

The teacher is often the very distraction which interrupts the learning process.[2] Inexperienced teachers often feel that in order to be truly successful, they must be the center of class attention. However, in the classroom there can be only one focal point, namely, the lesson. Competition for the attention of the students between the teacher and the lesson only results in diminished learning and increased problems of class control.

For example, beginning female teachers, in their attempt to make a good appearance and to seem truly professional, often inquire as to the proper length of a teacher's skirts. The answer should depend, of course, on the lady wearing the skirt. How shapely are her legs? Does she know how to sit and move around the classroom gracefully and modestly?

Adolescent boys are very easily distracted by a pair of attractive legs. In fact, they would much rather spend the entire class period staring at the teacher's legs than concentrating on their lesson. Such attention may be highly flattering to the teacher. It is unfortunate but true that some teachers require this type of attention to satisfy their own ego needs. But this attention should not be confused with an interest in learning nor be considered an effective method of teaching.

If the attention of the boys in class is controlled by the teacher's physical attractiveness, how will the girls react? It is highly

---

[2]For a discussion about teacher-problems see Arthur T. Jersild, *When Teachers Face Themselves* (New York: Teachers College Press, 1955).

probable that they will consider the teacher "competition" and begin to resent her presence. As a result, both the boys and girls will be alienated from the lesson and from learning.

Mannerisms (Did you see that?)   We all have mannerisms which are uniquely our own. In most cases, these actions are harmless because they prove no real distraction for the students. If, however, they become too pronounced or frequent during a class period, they may take precedence over the lesson.

Students have been known to count the number of times a teacher clears his throat (even to forming a betting pool as to the number of times within a class period), coughs, scratches his head, sniffs, kicks the leg of his desk as he walks by, says "And now boys and girls," and countless other idiosyncrasies that teachers, as human beings, possess.

Self-understanding and a realization by the teacher that *he* can be a distraction to his students and, in effect, a source of competition with the lesson being presented may eliminate some possible causes of classroom problems.

Playing back a tape-recording of the class is an excellent way to discover if there are any pet phrases that are being repeated over and over again, perhaps to the irritation of the students. Having an honest and diplomatic colleague unobtrusively observe the lesson may also reveal some previously unknown idiosyncrasy. An even more objective "audience" would be the video-tape recorder. The teacher could privately rerun the tape of his lesson for his own evaluation.

Planning (If you don't have a plan, the students will)   Proper planning is another factor which will assist in retaining the student's attention on the material under consideration. Although most teachers abandon the highly structured lesson plans which were required in the college methods courses the minute they enter their own classroom, they have, however, learned to make plans which they will find usable. This is the most important aspect of any lesson plan—its usability. Elaborately written plans which cannot be translated into effective lessons are of little value.

One of the immediate issues which the classroom teacher faces concerns the material to be taught. This requires both careful selection and examination. The beginning teacher, whose head has been crammed, over the years, with the knowledge of his discipline, often attempts to transfer this information *en toto* to his students. Obviously, such efforts are doomed to failure.

The new teacher must begin by setting realistic goals and determining precisely what he is attempting to accomplish in this classroom.[3] He should constantly ask himself "Why should students learn this now?" For if the teacher does not know what he is trying to accomplish in terms of the day's lesson, how will his students know what is expected of them? An aimless lesson is a direct invitation to classroom problems. The teacher must know where he is going, why, and how (what methods or techniques will be utilized) if he is to retain control of the class.

The question, however, of why any specific material should be studied cannot be answered solely by the instructor (a fact that far too many forget). The teacher in his planning for the course should structure the subject matter so that students will see its relevance and importance to them. But only the student can absorb the material; the teacher cannot learn it for him. Thus, the effective instructor feels it imperative to spend some time at the beginning of the school year explaining his goals; asking students for suggestions and reactions to his proposed program and modifying his original plans, if necessary. The final objectives, cooperatively determined, should therefore be clearly understood.

Goals and Motivation (Going my way?)   Frequently, however, the goals of students and teachers are not similar. The inexperienced secondary teacher need only think back to his recently completed student days to confirm this. What was his goal when he studied Geography II? Was it to secure a passing grade, or, as Professor Rock hoped, to analyze the significance of the earth's physical features? Then there were those elective courses taken as "fillers" to complete the required hours for the degree. These courses were not chosen to deepen aesthetic appreciations. No indeed. They were taken because they were considered snap courses or were given at a convenient time (or both, if the student was very lucky). So, if teachers themselves possessed somewhat questionable goals (and motives) when they were students, is it not possible (if not highly probable) that younger, less mature students are not in school for the sheer joy of learning? The successful teacher will attempt to learn the students' goals (discouraging as this may prove to be). Goals are usually as diverse as the students in the class. For some, the aim is to pass; others want to get an A; some study world history because

[3]For an exploration of goal-setting and preparing instructional objectives, see Robert F. Mager, *Preparing Instructional Objectives* (Palo Alto: Fearon Publishers, 1962).

it is required for college entrance; some want to speak a foreign language. Recognition of the real objectives and motives[4] of students can help immeasurably in determining the most effective teaching techniques.

Understanding the ability levels of his classes is also of paramount importance to the teacher in successful planning. Some schools group students heterogeneously; others attempt homogeneous groupings based on previous academic performance, standardized test scores, or other criteria. The teacher should check pertinent student data available in the Guidance Office; the counselor can provide additional information about his students. Unfortunately, some teachers use standardized test scores or previous grades as an excuse for poor teaching (or no teaching). "Have you seen that bunch of dumb-dumbs they've given me this year? No one could teach them anything. I'm not going to kill myself trying." Though overreliance on standardized test scores can be damaging, when used wisely they provide one more clue to the teacher in determining the potential of his students.

Teachers who fail to recognize the range of ability levels within their classes are courting frustration for themselves and their students. They must realize that they are no longer in a college situation where the work is assigned and then forgotten until it miraculously appears on the predetermined due date.

Teaching Techniques (How to make a point)   Unfortunately, the inexperienced teacher frequently enters the secondary school classroom having spent the preceding four years listening almost exclusively to a wide variety of lectures (including lectures on the evils of lecturing). It is possible that he may have heard some brilliant speakers. It is probable that he was exposed to some very dull ones. But the chances are strong that he has never questioned the actual teaching efficiency of the method itself. But is talking teaching? Is that all there is to it? Just tell 'em; that's it. Any new teacher who attempts a 45-minute lecture to a class of restless adolescents is quickly brought to the hard realization that to spellbind such an audience would require the skill of a Churchill and the stamina of a lion tamer. Furthermore, their short attention span almost precludes the use of such a procedure over an extended period of time.

So the choice of teaching techniques is of prime importance.

[4]For a broader examination of the nature of goals and motivation in learning see H. J. Klausmeier and William Goodwin, *Learning and Human Abilities,* 2d ed. (New York: Harper & Row, Publishers, 1966), Chap. 12.

Are the ones chosen really the best means available for making the lesson understood and for involving the student in learning? Must one start, for example, with the Pilgrim Fathers and trudge year by year, war by war, through 11th-grade American history, never quite making it to the 20th century? Is the too frequently heard defense of "Why, we've always taught that way" sufficient justification for continuing any particular method?

Strategies such as the inquiry-discovery method, simulation games, role playing, independent research, and field studies activate student interest. Creative use of audio-visual aids can breathe new life into a presentation. Critical thinking and self-expression can be encouraged through techniques emphasizing student interaction.

It should be remembered that all learners do not learn at the same rate. There may be 35 bodies in the classroom, but that does not assure that 35 minds are all marching along together. Individualizing instruction (much easier said than done, admittedly) would herald the end of the "shotgun" approach, favored by too many teachers, in which facts are fired at the entire class in the hope that some will hit a student or two who are prepared to receive them. The teacher who attempts to vary techniques and strategies must be conversant with learning theories, continuing to probe *how* students learn as well as *why*. A teacher confident of his knowledge will have the security necessary to explore and attempt new techniques. Imagination and variety hold the promise of teaching which could involve and excite students, encouraging them to think.

Flexibility is another key to successful teaching. If the planned lesson for the day appears to be ineffective (discussing the merits of the *Canterbury Tales* immediately following a vigorous pep rally), a wise teacher will change his approach to the topic. Or, occasionally abandoning the lesson planned for that day altogether and following a student interest or concern about another topic may prove more profitable. In this way, the teacher retains the attention of his students rather than see it shift into noneducational areas.

Sensitivity to the emotional climate in the classroom, recognizing changes in student mood and adjusting teaching strategies accordingly, facilitates teaching and learning. The successful teacher does not limit his responsibility to filling 150 "faceless" minds with facts on world history, math, or Elizabethan drama. If he is genuinely interested in reaching young minds, then his efforts transcend textual material and extend to understanding each learner as a unique individual, deserving of respect. He realizes that before students will respond to his efforts to communicate his knowledge, he must convey to them his acceptance of each of them (whether an A student or one who is barely passing), his intent to like each one and together create an atmosphere for effective learning.

The Academic Game (Passing) No teacher should keep secret the mechanical operation of his class. Students should know from the beginning of the year just what is expected of them. To a student, nothing is more frustrating than trying to guess what the teacher expects him to accomplish or how he is to behave. Far too often, teachers operate under the false assumption that students know what is expected of them. This is rarely the case unless they are told. Teacher demands from class to class differ widely. Students are entitled to know all of the requirements of the course and their individual responsibilities as members of the class. Naturally, this should include the basis on which grades will eventually be assigned, procedures for making up work when absent, rules regarding tardiness, and any behavioral taboos in the classroom.

When making assignments initially, teachers often fail to give proper consideration to the weight each activity will bring to the final grade. Unfortunately for the student, this decision is saved until the end of the term when the teacher is determining grades. The student then learns that an activity which he believed to be relatively insignificant in relation to the term's total work represented a large percentage of the final grade. There is a strong justification for students to question the fairness of the teacher's making this decision concerning grades so late.

The class should also know what to expect from the teacher. We all know that a teacher is expected to teach. But what does that mean in terms of achieving the instructional goals of the course? What is the role of the teacher? Is he to be the absolute, unquestioned source of wisdom, the leader, who will give all directions, control all activities? Or will he act as a guide for activities which will be primarily student-initiated? And the students? Are they to be passive little sponges, absorbing and regurgitating the facts presented to them? Or are they expected to do independent thinking and research and present their findings to the class? Will there be any retribution if the pupil's thinking appears to contradict the opinion of the teacher? Just how much responsibility does each student have toward the others in the class? Is each youngster expected to listen to presentations from his peers, even to learn from them as well as from his teacher? Is learning a cooperative process between teacher and students? Particularly in situations where the learner must assume a more active role, perhaps a quite unfamiliar one where he must be more responsible for his own learning, the teacher must plainly indicate this fact while fully explaining his own role in the teaching-learning process. The ground rules for profitable coexistence should be clearly set forth at the beginning of the school year.

The Behavioral Game (Surviving)   When we look to the actual functioning of the class, students want to know the rules and regulations under which they will exist. Unless the students have a sixth sense, a crystal ball, or highly developed ESP, it is grossly unfair to expect them to know without ever having been told what is required of them. The frustration and irritation they will undoubtedly feel and may express when caught in such a situation are understandable.

Whether the teacher alone establishes the rules for the class or whether they are decided by the entire class is determined by the teacher's own philosophy of classroom control. It should be remembered, however, that those rules which students establish themselves should be much easier to enforce than those which are imposed from above or which the students feel are oppressive or unfair. Of course, it must be accepted that some students will find *all* rules distasteful and will only grudgingly abide by them. This is where group determination of the rules can act as a force to guarantee acceptance.

In either case, a long set of rules may be considered a challenge by some students. Many teachers let the rules evolve naturally throughout the year as certain situations arise, feeling that until the problem occurs, there is no point in dealing with it. To some youngsters, however, this seems unfair, and they may petulantly complain, "You can't do that. You made all the rules in September. You can't add any more now." To which the teacher, with the agility of a Philadelphia lawyer, will counter that new problems require new solutions.

Some teachers who have pet peeves mention them at the beginning of the year and quite unequivocally assert that breaking this or that taboo will bring quick punishment to the offender. True, this may provide the class with a weapon to use against the teacher. But having been duly warned, the offending culprit can expect no mercy when finally caught. As a result, students usually will find other ways to brighten their days without resorting to the one "crime" from which they cannot hope to escape punishment by means of the ploy, "I didn't know that would upset you."

When rules are established, some provision must be made for those who violate the rules. This punishment must never be connected with the academic work of the class. It is a sad commentary on our educational philosophy that some teachers today still lower a student's academic grade for classroom misbehavior. This confusion between academic accomplishment and social deviation should be clarified. The assignment of extra school work—additional math problems or the copying of a poem several times—equates learning with punishment and has no place in our schools. The two are separate and distinct functions and should be treated as such. If teachers look upon learning as a form of punishment, how can they extol the pleasures and benefits of learning? Even the dullest student can detect the inconsistency, if not hypocrisy, of such thinking.

Rules and the necessary enforcement procedures must be realistic to the students and to the classroom situation. They must also be enforced in the same way for all students—the best student in the class as well as the perennial trouble-maker. New teachers, in their attempt to prod malingering students into doing their work on time, often fall into this kind of trap. An assignment date is set. *No* excuse for the work's being late will be accepted (short of the student's death). A late paper automatically receives a failing grade. Then what happens? The best student in the class (who always hands his work in early) becomes ill, or there is a death in his family, and the teacher is faced with enforcing a rule which was designed for an entirely different purpose and for an entirely different type of student. But what do we do in the face of such mitigating circumstances? Can we consider ourselves just, fair, humane if we penalize a child if his term paper is late because he had the flu? Children expect consistent treatment from a teacher, but like Shakespeare they recognize, too, that the quality of mercy is not strained. Students recognize the importance of rules and expect to be punished when they break a rule openly and with no reasonable excuse. They also have the right to expect that should mitigating circumstances be present, they will be given fair and equal consideration. This oftentimes puts an additional burden on the teacher (Solomon trying to determine where the truth lies in order to dispense justice). Students have a right to expect consistency from the teacher in dealing with each and every one of them, but *consistency is not rigidity.* At times teachers, in their sincere efforts to be impartial and fair, err in the other direction by accepting no excuses, listening to no explanations, and thus becoming unfair and intolerant in their attempt to be just.

Some teachers feel that it is often impossible to know the whole truth about a given situation and adopt a policy best described as keeping the students "loose." The reasoning goes something like this: "If the student does not know what to expect from me, he will be more alert and less inclined to try anything." Using this rationale, the teacher may appear to be Mr. Friendly on one day and Ivan the Terrible the next. Under this method of teaching, the role of the student can be compared to that of a yo-yo. He is constantly being jerked up during his dealings with the teacher. The student is placed in the unenviable position of trying to guess the mood of his teacher for that day. As you would imagine, he frequently misreads the signs. As a result, the student and the teacher often find themselves at odds over what actually may be insignificant matters simply because the student did not understand the teacher's mood or remarks. Eventually students recognize this approach and begin to resent it. They may decide that "what is sauce for the goose is sauce for the gander" and exhibit the same mercurial behavior towards the teacher— cooperative one day, like Hell's angels the next.

Just as teachers seek to understand what makes a student tick so that they can work more effectively with each child, so must the student understand his position when entering the teacher's classroom. When the teacher provides these guidelines, needless problems of classroom control will be avoided.

Students

Harmony in the classroom rests largely on *mutual* respect. Frequently secondary teachers are accused—at times with considerable justification—of an overconcern with subject matter. They do not want to become "involved" with their students as individuals; instead they see them only as little "fact machines" to be stuffed with appropriate data. Teachers who wish to be successful in the classroom must learn how to communicate with their students as individuals of worth. The first step in achieving effective communication requires the teacher to take the time and trouble to learn each student's name and to respect the dignity of each. We agree that this is not always easy, but it is necessary.

One of the surest ways to crush this dignity is to equate a student to an object. Teachers often call on a student by identifying him by the chair on which he is sitting, "You, fourth row, third seat." Respect breeds respect. The sooner each student's name is learned, the better will be the teacher's classroom control.

With this in mind, many teachers use an alphabetical seating chart until they have learned the names of their students. Then, if the teacher does not believe in maintaining seats in this way, or even in assigning seats on a permanent basis, he can permit the students to select their own seats in the room. It is interesting to note though that once a student has selected a seat, he considers it *his*, and pity any intruder. It is often surprising to see a high school junior or senior raging because "He took my seat" and expecting the teacher to evict the offender instantly.

Permitting students to select their own seats may be the best way to begin a school year. Although it might be easier for the teacher to learn the names of the students if they were seated in alphabetical order, this arrangement does not take into consideration those students who should sit in the front of the room because of sight or hearing difficulties. Many times these students will not ask the teacher for special placement and will take the assigned seat even if they will consequently have difficulty in following class activities. Should the teacher ask if anyone is having trouble hearing or seeing, the adolescent, painfully conscious of peer approval, will hesitate to admit he is in any way different. Alphabetical placement also assigns the same students to approximately the same location in each of their classes; names beginning with *A* are always seated in the front. The poor *W*s, *Y*s and *Z*s are relegated to the rear. Purely alphabetical arrangement will invariably place some six-foot two hulk of humanity in front of a petite five-foot lass, who may find the protective screen an excellent way to avoid any participation in the class.

The free choice arrangement can be extremely revealing to the teacher in organizing and conducting the class. He can see the natural interaction between students indicated by their choices, observe cliques and factions, and note if greater harmony is achieved within the class when the students select their own places. Also, giving students this freedom of choice places upon *them* the burden for responsible behavior.

Involvement with one's students, however, implies an effort beyond learning their names and observing interaction within the classroom. Some teachers seem totally unaware that students attend other classes or that there are extracurricular activities in which they participate. Some even fail to recognize their students outside the classroom. The face is identifiable only when it pops out from the second seat, third row. Nevertheless there is a world outside the teacher's classroom filled with activities that deserve his interest and participation.

Attending school functions will provide the teacher with greater insight into the real personalities of his students. He may find the quiet girl from 6th period is an accomplished actress starring in the school play. Complimenting Bill on his scoring at Friday's basketball game may not turn him into an *A* student in French, but it will strengthen the rapport between teacher and student. As a result of praising Bill's accomplishment and thus recognizing his importance in another area, Bill sees his teacher not as a drill master of irregular verbs, but an adult genuinely interested in and pleased by his success. Far too many teachers label a student dumb if he appears uninterested or is not succeeding in the course they teach. Few students are able to excel in every subject (few teachers, too, if the truth were known); yet they are talented in some areas. A teacher interested in his students helps them develop a secure self-image by accepting them as they are, by recognizing their strengths, allowing for their shortcomings, and working to realize their potential.

Students *do* have a life outside the school. Surprisingly enough some teachers feel that a student's personal life and his academic pursuits can remain totally separated. Failing to recognize that all behavior is caused by the interaction of a multitude of variables, they dissect students into little pieces labeled "home," "school," and "after school."

"But how can I know about 150 kids?" Or, "I don't parade *my* problems in the classroom; I won't permit my students to do it either." Or, "I haven't got time." These are all familiar refrains from teachers who believe learning is not influenced by outside factors. But like strawmen, these excuses are easily blown down. Teachers who understand their students are able to teach them more effectively.

The adolescent worried about a personal problem may find his studies of secondary importance. His apparent uninterest could mask fear and frustration. An insensitive teacher might unwittingly aggravate the situation. Suddenly pressure and worry explode. The student becomes a discipline problem.

Actually it is not so difficult to know one's students—if the teacher is willing to make the effort. During homeroom, the teacher who is sympathetic to the student returning after an illness, who remembers the student with an ill parent and inquires about him, is showing his interest in his pupils as human beings. The teacher who notices and comments when students wear new clothes, change their hairdo (or hair color) or get their Varsity letter also is saying, loud and clear, "I care about you; you are important." Praise or acknowledgment reaffirms the importance of the student as a person.

Equally important to a strong teacher-student relationship and the building of mutual respect is the teacher's willingness to listen to his students, to be available at times to serve as a sounding board for adolescent problems and ideas. Informal talk sessions enable the teacher to understand the world of his students. Usually they will respond positively to an adult evidencing genuine interest in them as individuals, not just names in a grade book.

Classrooms

When it comes to the physical properties of the classroom, the teacher has very little, if anything, to say about its location, size, ventilation, lighting, or furnishings. We inherit our rooms in a variety of conditions. It is true that a few years of seniority in a school will give a teacher some proprietary rights on a certain classroom. Because of this, many times the new teacher will find himself designated as a "floater." He is a teacher without a permanent room to call his own, forced to move to several classrooms during the course of the school day. If he plays his cards right, he may earn the privilege of using one drawer in the desk in each room (naturally, it will be the bottom drawer and have a tendency to stick). This in no way gives one a sense of belonging or enjoying any rights of tenancy. He soon comes to realize that having a room of his own is a very special privilege earned by successful service on the front lines. When, finally, he receives a room of his own, it may develop that it must be shared for part of the day with some unknown and probably unreliable floater. Even so, that does not prohibit him from making the best out of a sometimes poor situation. Floaters and permanent residents can work cooperatively to keep the room looking as inviting as possible.

Location and size of an individual room are beyond a teacher's control. Some of the other physical properties of the room, however, can be altered by the teacher. A classroom must be aired out periodically during the course of the day so that it does not become musty, stagnant, and unpleasant. If the room is too warm, the class may become sluggish and inattentive. If it is too cold, the major concern of the students will shift from the lesson to an attempt to maintain a comfortable body temperature. The teacher will quickly learn that opening and closing windows seems to be one of the consuming interests of some of his students and he may find himself acting as a temperature-control warden. For as soon as John (loudly complaining of impending suffocation) throws open all of the windows, Mary moans that she is being frozen to death. A lively exchange of opinion between the two and other interested onlookers can quickly result.

Classroom lighting is another area of physical importance. No class can function adequately if the lighting is poor. It is the teacher's responsibility to try to assure all students in the room sufficient light for working. Teachers often neglect those students at the opposite end of the room from the windows and tend to feel that natural lighting from the windows is adequate for all areas of the classroom. Teachers who move around to all sections of the room as they teach, however, are more likely to be aware of any drastic differences in both lighting and temperature.

Moving about the room will also disclose that some of the students nearest to the windows are taking advanced courses in knot tying, using the venetian blind cords for practice materials. Untying their elaborate creations can be a source of great frustration to the unwary teacher (particularly should he not discover this pastime until he wishes the blinds closed to show a film and requires five minutes to untangle the cord). Teachers sometimes reach the point of forbidding *anyone* to touch the blinds. Naturally they are then accused of being heartless, ruthlessly trying to blind innocent students with the glare of the noonday sun as it strikes their desks. Also, as the warmer weather arrives, some students will complain that the sun is so hot they are likely to suffer third degree burns. Again, a contest can develop between the blind openers and the blind closers. (Remember, closing the blinds blocks the flow of air into the room.) Protagonists from both camps are likely to pop up at any given moment to rearrange the offending shade. This sudden movement can disrupt even the most smoothly organized class. If not the movement itself, then certainly the complaints of those who oppose the action taken will bring learning to a standstill. Again, the teacher who frequently circulates around the classroom can prevent these occurrences by checking on the light and temperature at different times of the day.

Newer schools have made great improvements in the physical attractiveness of the classroom through the use of pastel paints, brightly colored furniture, and even carpeting. In older schools, however, teachers often have to combat institutional dreariness.

This is not to imply that a student cannot learn in a dreary setting—but why should he have to? A student should feel that his classroom is a place conducive to work. The classroom can reflect a spirit of warmth, of "caring" on the part of the teacher, which will help to convey the teacher's concern for the comfort and well-being of his students. Keeping a room attractive can also offer excellent opportunities to teach students social responsibility and self-discipline. The way the classroom is maintained indicates how much esprit de corps the students and teacher feel toward each other and the school. The teacher who cares enough to bring in bright bulletin board materials (often paid for from his own funds) will soon find his efforts rewarded and reciprocated when students respond and bring in something which they feel would improve *their* room. Not only is the physical appearance of the room heightened but the emotional and learning climate is also strengthened.

Summary

In these few pages, we have attempted to develop a perspective on the nature of discipline and the factors which impede an effective learning climate. We have illustrated how the teacher himself sometimes is a distracting influence, drawing the attention of his students from the lesson to himself. Failure on the part of the teacher to set realistic goals for his students and to plan effective lessons also invites disorder in the classroom.

The teacher must further recognize his responsibilities concerning the physical environment of his classroom. The room should be a cheerful, comfortable place in which to teach and learn. Students should feel an atmosphere of acceptance in the classroom where each is considered an important, contributing member.

Mutual respect between teacher and student must be developed. A teacher's failure to recognize the dignity and worth of each student can quickly cause serious discontent among the students. Successful teaching under such conditions becomes extremely difficult, if not impossible.

Furthermore, the teacher who fails to advise his students of the rules and their responsibilities in his class is asking for trouble. Frustrated students are likely to strike back against the source of their frustration with hostile and disruptive behavior.

In this chapter, the necessity for devising guidelines under which both teacher and student can operate successfully has been explored. The following chapters will investigate in greater detail how a variety of specific problems originate and the action options that are available to the teacher for resolving them.

Suggested Readings

Blount, Nathan S., and Klausmeier, Herbert J. *Teaching in the Secondary School.* 2d ed. New York: Harper & Row, Publishers, 1968. Chap. 6, 7, 8, 9, 11. Discusses teaching methods, techniques, and procedures for lesson and unit planning.

Carlson, Elliot. *Learning Through Games.* Washington, D.C.: Public Affairs Press, 1969. Develops the background of learning through games as a new approach in problem solving. Presents examples of actual game situations for classroom use.

Clark, Leonard H. and Starr, Irving S. *Secondary School Teaching Methods.* New York: The Macmillan Company, 1967. Chap. 4. Explores the importance of setting the "right" emotional climate in the classroom and the limitations of punishment in achieving classroom control.

Filbin, Robert L., and Vogel, Stefan. *So You're Going to be a Teacher.* Great Neck: Barron's Educational Series, Inc., 1962. Examines reasons for choosing teaching, rewards, problems, including a framework for classroom control with special emphasis on the junior high school.

Gnagey, William J. *The Psychology of Discipline in the Classroom.* New York: The Macmillan Company, 1968. Brief discussion, with practical classroom application, of operant conditioning in controlling deviant behavior.

Grambs, Jean D., Carr, John C. and Fitch, Robert M. *Modern Methods in Secondary Education.* 3d ed. New York: Holt, Rinehart & Winston, Inc., 1970. Explores the role of the teacher, the nature of the adolescent, resources, teaching techniques, planning strategies, barriers to teacher-student communication, and democratic discipline.

Hoffman, Banesh. *Tyranny of Testing.* New York: P. F. Collier, Inc., 1962. Explores the weaknesses of standardized testing and the dangers of overreliance on and misuse of test scores.

Horn, Gunner; Franklin, Marian; Kendrick, Alexander; and Goldberger, Paul. "Some Thoughts about Teachers and Teaching." *Today's Education* 59, No. 1 (January, 1970) : 12–18. Four statements about teachers, their role in the classroom, and their effect on their students, stressing the importance of teacher involvement.

Mager, Robert E. *Developing Attitude Toward Learning.* Palo Alto: Fearon Publishers, 1968. Discusses effectiveness of good planning, including setting of objectives and maintaining environment conducive to learning.

Postman, Neil and Weingartner, Charles. *Teaching As a Subversive Activity.* New York: Dell Publishing Co., Inc., 1969. An indictment of present-day teaching practices and discussion of new approaches to teaching, learning, and determining relevance of subject matter.

Thomas, R. Murray. *Aiding the Maladjusted Pupil: A Guide for Teachers.* New York: David McKay Co., Inc., 1967. Chap. 4. A discussion of various ways in which the student's environment can be changed to aid in his adjustment.

2

Teacher-Caused Problems

There are times when the teacher himself is the cause of many of the discipline problems which occur in his classroom. Sometimes his own actions—or his reactions to various situations—openly invite further trouble. He is the one who determines the direction which will be taken. Furthermore, the action option which the teacher selects to solve a particular problem has repercussions that extend beyond the parties involved. Nothing that a teacher does relating to classroom discipline lives and dies in isolation. The action option chosen to meet a situation will not take place in a vacuum. Whatever a teacher does has an effect not only on the offending student or students, but on his relationship with the entire class. With this in mind, our first bit of advice would have to be: don't look for trouble; it will find you fast enough!

Now what exactly does that mean? Teachers are horrified when they are accused of searching for trouble. Perhaps the following will illustrate our point. We have all heard students say ironically, "You should just try to get away with anything in Mr. X's class. Boy, he'll stomp on you!" Mr. X would appear to be a teacher with firm control over his class. But this interpretation fails to take into account the nature of the adolescent. The temptation to try to get away with "anything" is at times just too irresistible to ignore (especially for boys). This feeling on the part of the student is very natural. But what should the teacher do? If the infraction is minor, it might best go unnoticed by the teacher. Let the students win every now and then. It cannot really hurt the teacher, and it may satisfy the students' desire for a victory over an adult. The teacher's ire should be reserved for important matters.

Unfortunately there are some teachers, however, who feel that a student's failure to abide by each and every rule should be duly noted and dealt with summarily and firmly. They honestly believe that each student violation of a rule brings the school just one step closer to anarchy and, therefore, that each incident must be nipped in the bud. Far too often additional trouble of a significant nature arises after a teacher has verbally pounced on a student, denouncing him before the entire class for his failure to comply with a teacher or with a school-made regulation. Such teachers feel that *naturally* there can be no mitigating circumstances.

By courting trouble, teachers may lose sight of the real reasons that the student is in school. The strict observation of each and every rule without exception often wastes class time and appears somewhat ridiculous to students. Teachers who demand such rigid conformity should question their own motives. Are they afraid to deal on an individual basis with students, and do they, therefore, hide behind the protection of an impersonal set of regulations? Does enforcing rules provide them with a sense of power or superiority that they need to bolster their self-image?

For example, some teachers take pride in never admitting a student into the classroom after the final bell has rung. Their students know, when they find themselves still outside the classroom (for whatever reason) when the bell has finished ringing, not even to attempt to enter the room. They must first go to the office and obtain a Late Admit slip. Of course, on the way to the office they will probably be intercepted by another equally zealous teacher who will cross-examine them as to why they are in the hall without a hall pass. This excursion from the classroom (hall interrogation by a teacher) to the office (office interrogation by a member of the administrative staff) and back to the classroom (teacher interrogation as to the *real* reason for being late) will cost the student a considerable amount of class time. But the student will have learned a lesson. That is, he has learned that a rule is a rule . . . (and a good way to get out of class).

This should be the end of such an incident, but it usually isn't. Once the offending student is inside the classroom, some teachers will then spend valuable class time castigating the unspeakable culprit who was not in his seat when the bell rang. A tirade on such a matter is not likely to produce the appropriate learning climate for the remainder of the period.

Rules are necessary only insofar as they aid the teaching-learning situation. Rules for the sake of rules will actually interfere with the teaching-learning climate of the classroom. If a teacher with the aid of his students determines the few ground rules necessary to govern the classroom at the beginning of the school year, the students will then know what is expected of them. Work can begin when the bell rings without further unnecessary delay. On those few occasions when the students are not ready to begin their work, waiting quietly until they come to order can prove far more effective than creating a scene merely because one or two students were not primed and ready for action. Making a scene is exhausting for the teacher and totally irritating to the students.

It's Not What You Say: It's How You Say It

The teacher's tone of voice gives eloquent clues to his true feelings toward his subject matter and students. If the teacher sounds bored, why should his students feel differently? *Enthusiasm is catching.* A teacher who is excited about his subject matter will find that many students will be affected by his own excitement.

Teachers who speak in a monotone have been known to reduce a class to semiconsciousness in a remarkably short period of time. The teacher who mumbles will irritate and frustrate the student who wants to listen while unwittingly providing a soothing background for the less-motivated student seeking a nap.

A teacher who is not a native of the particular geographic area in which he is teaching and has a midwestern twang or a southern drawl, or is a New England *r*-dropper, may be mercilessly mimicked by some of his students. A sense of humor can offset much of this kind of trouble, plus some careful attention to correcting those speech patterns found distracting to students.

Yet, the effective use of one's voice—developing the skill of changing volume, tempo, and rhythm at the right moment—is very important in retaining the attention of the class. Such voice manipulation can emphasize, embellish, and effectively convey the teacher's feelings about the subject matter and become the key to regulating class activity.

The teacher who declares that he always loves all of his students (a totally unbelievable concept) while consistently employing a patronizing or belligerent tone of voice quickly betrays his true emotions. Many situations which occur in the classroom receive unnecessary emphasis and impetus by the tone of voice employed by the participants, both teacher and students. Frequently it is not what was said by the teacher to a student or student to a teacher but rather how it was said that becomes the crux of the matter.

Unfortunately, some teachers find it difficult to use a firm tone when necessary with students (a tone which is not patronizing, belligerent, or sarcastic). There are definite times when such a tone is not only required but expected by the students. Students are wise. They know only too well when they have exceeded the limits of propriety, and they expect a firm teacher reaction. Do not disappoint them.

Miss Adams, a first-year teacher of 10th-grade biology, was anxious to have her students like her. She tried not to raise her voice in anger or show any signs of disapproval regardless of the students' behavior. Because of her lack of control of students in the classroom, it became increasingly difficult for her to teach. Eventually the situation had reached such a state that she was finally begging her students to be quiet and pay attention, but they just ignored her.

In situations like this, a whining, pleading voice only serves as an invitation to chaos in the classroom.

Teachers, Too, Have Survival Needs

It should also be remembered that every teacher establishes those individual requirements which he feels are necessary for his survival in class. While some are necessary for student safety (as in science labs), others facilitate paper handling for the teacher. These procedures, which may be contrary to the requirements established by other teachers, can cause unwary students considerable frustration and consternation. Yet if teachers would take the time to explain why they want things done in a certain way, the rules might appear more reasonable to students.

Does it make any difference if students write in pencil or pen?

In mathematics, it is easier for students to erase errors made in pencil. But essays written in pen are easier for the English or social studies teacher to read. However, there are times when certain requirements, under close examination, seem rather petty.

For instance, why does Mr. B. insist on three-hole notebook paper, while the science teacher, Miss L., demands two-hole paper with wide spaces between the lines? Why must bibliographic reference cards for social studies term papers be done on 3-x-5 cards while the English teacher insists on the 4-x-6 size? What is the reason why students' names must be placed in the upper right corner of the French papers, the paper then folded lengthwise, while the math teacher demands unfolded sheets with the names placed in the upper left corner?

Teachers are human and have their personal likes and dislikes which at times they impose upon their students. These often vary greatly from teacher to teacher and seemingly defy logic and reason. In some classrooms, for example, gum chewing is almost a hanging offense. Other teachers are tolerant of gum chewing as long as the student does not blow bubbles or "snap" it. So the bright students quickly learn the idiosyncrasies of each of their five or six teachers (they "psych" the teacher), and with surprisingly good humor they acquire a chameleon-like ability to change their personalities to suit the demands of the teacher. In fairness to students, teachers should periodically reexamine their list of regulations to make sure they are necessary.

Where Are You Vulnerable?

When it comes to the fine art of classroom survival, students are not stupid. In fact, they are very wise—that is, teacher-wise. Thus, enterprising students soon learn that some teachers can be manipulated and provoked to such a point that the teacher loses control of himself and the class and thereby permits a crisis to develop. They could tell you, if you were to ask, which teacher will almost climb the wall if someone is whispering in class, and, conversely, which teacher will allow a noise level that would rival a world series crowd at fevered pitch.

It does not take students long to discover that women, as a rule, will take things which are said to them much more personally than will men. Rough or offensive language may prove so threatening—and be considered such an affront to her self-image —that a woman teacher may be rendered incapable of coping with the culprit.

Mrs. Webster was in charge of the study hall when Tom walked in late. She asked him why he was tardy and he did not answer her. She repeated the question and he then said, "It's none of your business, you old bitch." She was so startled, she couldn't reply and left the room, bringing the principal back to deal with Tom.

The male teacher's ego might be threatened by the reluctant adolescent who does not respond to a direction immediately or who mutters "try and make me." This apparent defiance may be considered by the teacher a challenge which must be met in a forceful (even physical) manner if he is to retain his image of authority. While men teachers often overreact to what they consider a transgression in manners by their male students, the same behavior by girls may receive no response. But should the teacher comment on her misbehavior, a pretty teenage miss who knows how (and, of course, when) to ply her feminine wiles will doubtless escape his wrath.

Maintaining Student Dignity

Although some teachers like many rules because they feel it makes their job much safer, too many rules can have a corrosive effect on the student's sense of his own worth. They make him feel that his individuality is being threatened or attacked and that he, as a person, is of little consequence in the scheme of adult life. In reaction to this feeling, a student may deliberately do something to be noticed and receive some attention. Granted, the recognition that he receives may not be of the most pleasant nature, but at least someone finally knows that he exists.

The problem of alienation is often more severe in our larger secondary schools. Students feel lost in a sea of faces. Their needs and expectations go unrecognized because of the large numbers of students involved. Should the student be shy or nondescript, he may go unnoticed by the teacher in a large classroom. Then, once in the halls, he is engulfed in the mass of humanity that shuffles from class to class.

His peer relationships may be sharply limited by the brief and impersonal encounters fostered by the size of the school. As a result, he finds his educational experience lonely and may seek recognition and approval of his classmates by deviant behavior.

Some teachers fail to recognize this in adolescents and further aggravate their sense of isolation by using their names as a means of control rather than of identification. There are teachers who persist in using only the student's last name, stating that this is the most effective way to remind the student that they mean business. This brisk, impersonal method relegates the student to the status of an object instead of a person.

Other teachers, as a Christmas present each year, call students by their first names (like petting a dog occasionally!). Then there are those teachers who use the titles *Mr.* and *Miss* with adolescents in an effort to make them grow up and respond like adults (a psychological and physiological impossibility).

In some cases, teachers insist on addressing students by their official names, ignoring the fact that Theodore may prefer to be called Ted; Bettie despises the name Elizabeth; and that Percy has always been known as Butch. It seems strange that teachers would object to something so important to the adolescent as his name, whatever he wants to be called. What real difference could it possibly make to the teacher unless it is a demonstration of power? However, to the student, it is a rejection of the image he wishes to create or of the person he believes himself to be.

One of the seemingly little things that many teachers have difficulty doing is pronouncing their students' names correctly. Errors in stressing the proper syllable are not deliberate. And considering the many students a teacher faces daily, it is understandable that some names would cause him trouble. Yet, at the same time, a student does not find the mispronunciation of his name before the class a light matter. Teachers should therefore make every effort to pronounce names correctly. An aid in accomplishing this is to write the name as it sounds in the role book next to the way it is actually spelled.

Public vs. Private Confrontations (Now or later?)   Though students strive to preserve their individuality, they also function during the major part of each school day as a member of a group. They are sensitive to any action by the teacher which would impair their position before their peers. Unfortunately, some teachers may fail to consider the interpersonal relationships of the class in their overconcern with subject matter. Therefore expression of the irritation they feel toward the student who delays class progress sometimes is not deferred until a more appropriate time but they display their ire before the entire class to the embarrassment and humiliation of the student.

The Third Degree (Confess!)   Any student who has ever been subjected to the third-degree technique can easily appreciate the fine skill which some teachers have attained in using this ego-deflating procedure. In some classes, the student who is late or forgets his homework is grilled with the sometimes frightening, almost sadistic, technique used by the bad guy in a spy thriller. The questions usually begin mildly enough, but this is often only a tactic used to create a false sense of security in the victim until the teacher is ready to draw in the net and land his fish. But why do teachers need to do this? Is it a form of student-baiting designed to demonstrate the teacher's superiority? Could it be an immature compulsion to have the last word? Or is the teacher honestly unaware that he is conducting an inquisition?

For example, after John has indicated that he cannot answer No. 3 from last night's homework because he does not have it with him, he is asked by his teacher (who appears genuinely concerned), "Why not, John?" The usual response is, "I left it home." Common sense would indicate that the teacher proceed with the lesson and speak with John later. But many teachers are unable to bypass such a marvelous opportunity to make the student squirm. So the fun begins.

"Are you *sure* you left it home?" Now it dawns on poor John that either his teacher is psychic or possesses some sixth sense and knows that he did not do his homework in the first place. He is also aware by this time that the attention of the entire class is concentrated on him. He wants off the hook—and quickly— unless he feels that a few exciting minutes of teacher-baiting are in order before he throws in the towel. "Well, I didn't do it," he sheepishly admits, hoping that the fatal blow will be fast and painless. But no such luck. "Didn't do it? I thought that you said that you had left it at home, John. Now, which is it?" demands his teacher, using his best confused look.

John blows it again. He is desperate by this time and willing to try anything. "Well, I didn't understand it. That's why I couldn't do it." "Didn't understand it, John? Just what didn't you understand about the assignment? Perhaps I can help you," replies his teacher.

"Well, ah, it's rather hard to explain." But his teacher insists that he try. "We all want to know why you were unable to understand the assignment when everyone else found it perfectly clear." Of course, by this time John would like to find a nice quiet hole, climb in, and pull it in after him. He has lost the skirmish and he knows it. The class knows it. The teacher knows it. "Perhaps you didn't even try to do it. Isn't that it?" probes the teacher. By this time John would even admit to the burning of Rome if he could sit down. So he declares what his teacher knew from the beginning, "I didn't even look at it."

It is now time for the coup de grace. "I'm certain, John, that this won't happen again, will it?" A miserable and bitterly angry John completely capitulates with a weak "No" and slides into his seat. Victory for the teacher? The entire class has been duly impressed (intimidated or angered) by the episode. The teacher may feel eminently satisfied with his skill in putting a prevaricator in his place, but he may discover that he has paid a high price for such shaky security. Certainly his relationship with John and the remainder of the class will be affected. The antagonism stirred up by such tactics may manifest itself in many different ways. John will not quickly forget his embarrassment at the hands of his teacher nor will he be inspired to do his homework. The teacher demonstrated his skill at verbal riposte at the expense of another. This is the lesson the class will remember. Furthermore, the interrogation wasted precious class time which should have been devoted to learning.

The teacher sincerely interested in discovering why John did not do his work would arrange a conference with him at a mutually convenient time. Then the teacher should listen to his explanation of why he was not able to get the work done. There could be many valid reasons, reasons which John might prefer not to divulge before the entire class. Unfortunately, teachers sometimes begin these conferences with such a negative attitude that the student lapses into defensive silence. The teacher, consequently, learns absolutely nothing about the real reasons for the failure to do the required work and may erroneously conclude the student is sullen or lazy or just doesn't care.

> Mr. Boland was talking to Mary about her failure to do homework in physical science. "Well, Mary, what have you got to say for yourself? This is the third time you haven't done your homework and you aren't even paying attention in class. You aren't going to pass if you keep this up. Well?" "You see, Mr. Boland," answered Mary, "I've just gotten this job from 4 to 9 P.M. and . . ." "Don't tell me about any job, Mary; school comes first with me and it should with you, too." Mary was about to add that she had to take the job because her father had just been laid off at the steel plant, but, noting Mr. Boland's attitude, said nothing more. Mr. Boland concluded the conference by warning Mary that job or no job if she didn't do her homework, he would fail her.

Thus even a teacher conscientious enough to arrange a student conference can defeat the purpose of the meeting by failing to listen and understand.

Search and Seizure (Hands up!)   Because a person is classified as a student does not mean that he has surrendered his personal liberties. Some teachers feel justified in demanding that students empty their pockets or handbags when valuable items have been reported missing in the classroom. Sometimes this also has been done to find contraband such as cigarettes, switchblade knives, and the like. Doubtless these same teachers would seek legal redress if they were themselves treated in a similar manner. Yet they feel perfectly justified in subjecting their students to this degrading and highly questionable procedure.

Another dangerous area for teachers involves seizure.[1] That is, after they have found a taboo item (a switchblade knife, for example), what gives the teacher the right to confiscate it? We have yet to find a teacher who has issued a receipt for an item taken from a student. Whatever is taken usually vanishes until the teacher finds it within his heart (often on the last day of school) to return the student's "toy."

Most often the article taken from a student is a magazine, book, or portable radio that the teacher feels is distracting the student and those seated around him from the lesson. Teachers need to ask themselves why students are interested in something other than the subject under classroom discussion. If they did, they might find that such items are brought to school for use during extended periods of boredom. If lessons were effective in developing student motivation, much of the contraband would disappear on its own accord.

Whatever the reason for these forbidden articles in the classroom, usually the student yields his treasure meekly. But one wonders at the legal implications of the entire process. What if he said "no"? Would the teacher feel within his rights to take the item by force? What if the student resisted, claiming that the teacher had no right to his property?

Before demanding that a youth surrender a possibly expensive item, such as a portable radio, a teacher should be certain that he does, in fact, have the authority to make such a demand. Furthermore, unless he has exercised good judgment and put it in the school safe, is he legally responsible for its replacement should the radio be broken or lost while in his possession? In this day and age, students are much more aware of their rights than ever before. Perhaps it is time that teachers also became aware

[1]For a discussion of student rights concerning such procedures, see the discussion/action draft by John Roemer, Executive Director, American Civil Liberties Union of Maryland, "A Bill of Rights for High School Students." (Mimeographed, undated).

of these rights.[2] Such awareness could avoid considerable embarrassment and trouble at a later date.

Another way in which a teacher can fan the fires of discontent in his own classroom is to become an active participant in the game of note interception. There are three major rules under which teachers can play this game. First, some teachers will, after they intercept a note, read its contents aloud to the entire class. This is designed to embarrass the student and discourage further note passing. At times, however, it is the teacher who is more embarrassed.

> Sally was caught passing a note in health class. Despite her protests, her teacher, Miss Prentiss, insisted she read it to the class. Looking very embarrassed, Sally read aloud "What would that old hag know about premarital sex. No man would ever be that desperate." The entire class, with the exception of Miss Prentiss, roared.

A second technique used is to tear up the note while commenting rather sarcastically about people who have so much time on their hands that they can write notes and still learn the material being covered. Or the teacher might comment that the student thinks he is so intelligent that he does not have to listen to what is going on in the class (this usually brings laughter from the other students). The third procedure is somewhat extreme. The student is informed that the note will be sent to his parents for their analysis (all the poor kid can hope for in this case is that the topic of his note was something inane).

All these actions are blatant invasions of privacy and are designed to humiliate the student before his peers and his teacher. Any teacher resorting to such procedures should ask himself if the end justified the means. He should also examine his own behavior in this situation. Was it curiosity, stupidity, or a need to assert dominance which motivated him? Occasional note passing is not such a grievous sin, and often it disturbs only the teacher. It is not really meant to be a personal affront and should not be taken as such.

Handling (Hands off!)   Some teachers appear to be unable to keep their hands to themselves. Teachers who indulge in these activities are likely to insist that "the kid knows that I'm just

[2]American Civil Liberties Union of Maryland, *Academic Freedom in the Secondary Schools* (New York: American Civil Liberties Union, 1969).

giving him a friendly pat." Now just what is a "friendly pat?" Why is it necessary to touch a student at all?

Unfortunately, there are teachers who enjoy touching their students. Some male teachers are unable to resist patting, pinching, or touching their attractive female students. These individuals quickly establish a dubious reputation for their slight-of-hand escapades. Few adolescent girls will complain officially about such treatment, thinking that few adults would believe a student. This does not, however, stop the molested girl from informing her friends (or occasionally her parents) about "Mr. Hands." When this happens, his effectiveness in the classroom has ended. No one respects a "dirty old man" and that is exactly what he becomes in the eyes of his students, male and female alike.

Not only are such teachers immature (perhaps even sick); they make themselves appear ridiculous, and they are courting an ugly scandal. Many an adolescent girl has imagined that her handsome teacher was romantically interested in her. As a result, she needs very little encouragement to envision that he reciprocates her feelings. A friendly pat or touch may be all that is required to reinforce what she wishes to believe. Should she relate her fantasies and the teacher's behavior to her parents or friends, it would become extremely difficult and embarrassing for the teacher to explain his actions. What was considered harmless can thus backfire with possibly tragic and often far-reaching complications.

Touching (Did that really hurt?)   Boys frequently find themselves on the receiving end of teacher power. There are times when a teacher will poke or push a student to hurry him along the hallway or down an aisle of the classroom. Teachers also poke students in the arm or chest when making a point about something under discussion. Although it is claimed that nothing is meant by these actions, there may be a considerable degree of force behind these "good-natured" pokes. The motives of the teacher and the reaction of the student bear careful scrutiny. Just why does a teacher resort to this particular means of dealing with students? Could it be possible that there is anger behind those supposedly friendly taps and punches?

For example, many male teachers like to pat a disruptive student on the head using the hand on which they are wearing their heavy college ring. Anyone who has experienced this knows it hurts. It is meant to hurt. However, in the adolescent culture one does not react to pain inflicted by a teacher. So the teacher meaning to hurt the student grins as he pats the offending boy's head; the boy grins as though he did not feel a thing.

Another technique employed along this same line could best be termed "the subtle pinch." The teacher places his hand "affectionately" on the shoulder of the offending male student. As the teacher speaks, he slowly begins to squeeze the student's shoulder muscle. To anyone passing by, the proceedings appear friendly enough. Usually both teacher and student manage to smile—after all, that is part of the game. The teacher gently increases the pressure and the student pretends that he feels nothing. (In some schools today, however, the teacher would very likely be slugged for such actions.)

At times teachers are quite open in their physical abuse of students. Many actually believe (or so they say) that hitting or shaking a student does the student a world of good. If a teacher were being completely honest with himself, he would have to admit that such actions only help to relieve his own frustrations. Any help which the student receives through these actions is purely accidental.

Although students rarely complain about these various techniques (perhaps they should complain more), the teacher has left himself wide open for trouble. What would happen if the student reciprocated such actions with equal or greater force? Does anyone seriously believe that the teacher would take what he gives with the apparent good humor shown by students? If not, then the teacher is taking advantage of some supposed immunity that forbids students from defending themselves. This would make the teacher a bully, wouldn't it? It would also indicate that his self-image is insecure and that he creates opportunities to prove his masculinity.

The likelihood of a student defending himself against teacher violence is increasing. Television brings riots, burnings, even murders into the intimacy of the home for all to view. Then the adolescent sees teachers (who are often his behavioral models) resort to violence to maintain their status. Thus violence seems legitimized and some adolescents will rationalize their use of the same tactics to achieve their ends.

A punch in the nose from a student may be the least of the problems experienced by a teacher who cannot keep his hands to himself. If one of his pushes or punches should cause a student to fall and injure himself, the teacher's career and financial security could vanish within a brief, careless moment.

The entire matter of teachers touching students is so dangerous and open to misunderstanding that the teacher should beware of putting himself in jeopardy. Yet, at times, especially when dealing with younger adolescents, teachers feel that touching the student is not only appropriate but necessary. A warm arm around the shoulder or an encouraging pat on the back signify acceptance or understanding. The key to touching a student should be the situation, the student himself, and the teacher's motives.

Sarcasm (Cut, cut)   Some insecure teachers consider sarcasm to be their thing. They have developed their skill in using a verbal knife to the point that they can skin a student without spilling a single drop of blood. As a technique, sarcasm is perhaps the most widely used method of control because it is so available.

When teachers talk about their use of this pointed weapon in chastising students, they usually say, "Oh, the kids know that I'm really just joking with them." Or, "Hank doesn't care what I say to him in class; he knows that I don't mean it." Yet if a student were to use the same tone of voice or words as the teacher, he would undoubtedly be sent to the principal's office with an angry note citing the youngster's impudent behavior.

Students question this double standard, and rightfully so. Just as the teacher seeks respect from the class, so does the student seek respect from the teacher. The class is composed of his peers with whom he associates during much of his social and academic life. He has every right to want them to respect him. Any attempt by the teacher to diminish his prestige will necessitate some action on his part to retain his status. Therefore it is important for teachers to weigh their words so as not to offend their students needlessly. By a battle of words the teacher alienates not only the student involved but the remainder of the class as well.

Being perfectly honest with ourselves, we will admit that sarcasm is meant to hurt, to sting. And whether we acknowledge it or not, when we use it against a student, there is some anger behind our words and a conscious attempt on our part to "put that kid in his place." In effect, we purposely and destructively set out to reduce his self-image and his position with his peer group. Of course it must be admitted that often teachers are unaware that their remarks are interpreted by students as sarcastic. However, the end result is the same.

If a teacher feels that he must chastise a student, he should do so in private. Even here, sarcasm is unnecessary and will hinder rather than aid the discussion.

Nagging (Say it again)   Although not as devastating a weapon as sarcasm, continual nagging by a teacher also can have an ego-diminishing effect on students. Teachers harp on the darndest things sometimes. Some teachers cannot stand to see a student idle. That is, they think the student is doing nothing. When this happens the teacher begins: "Don't you have anything to do?" "Are you using your time wisely?" "Your grades don't indicate that you have any time to spare?" Ad nauseam.

This brings to mind two factors that teachers are prone to forget. Students can learn their subject matter (English, history, math, etc.) in a time period other than the one in which the class period has been scheduled. Combined with the second factor— students may not appear to be doing anything when in fact they are reflecting upon some idea (a novel concept in education)— and, therefore, they may seem idle to the teacher. In both cases the teacher will accomplish very little by nagging the student. When left on their own, students will often pleasantly surprise their teachers by the responsibility they will assume and the quality of work they will produce. On the other hand extensive daydreaming may be symptomatic of a psychological problem, and the teacher should be sensitive to such a possibility.

> The students were talking in little groups before the start of the English class. Pat came in but spoke to no one. She arranged her books in a neat stack and seemed completely absorbed. After the bell rang, though her notebook was opened, she did not take any notes, did not volunteer any answers and seemed to be paying no attention to the lesson. The English supervisor who was observing Mr. Reidel's class asked him at the end of the period about the girl's apparent disinterest. "Oh, Pat, never participates; in fact she hasn't spoken one word to me for the past month. I've tried to get her to participate but she won't even answer. It's like she's in another world. She's failing but she doesn't cause any trouble, so I just let her alone."

Unfortunately, some teachers do not recognize the student who is literally withdrawing from reality; instead they dissipate their energies in nagging students about trivial infractions of rules. Talking and gum chewing are two good examples. Yet an occasional whispered remark from student to student will not disrupt the class nor will the silently moving jaws of the quiet gum-chewer. Why then do these offenses bother some teachers so much? Obviously it cannot be such trivial actions themselves. The issue is really not one of bad behavior but rather one of the teacher's level of tolerance. How much leeway will he allow a student, how much freedom to learn in his own environment?

Another form of nagging, which is particularly irritating to students, occurs when a student feels that he is being singled out for unnecessary attention. This is the day when he is unable to do anything right and the teacher catches him doing everything wrong. He is called down for slamming his books on the desk (they really slipped). He is caught borrowing paper for the assignment (his brother took the last few pages from his notebook before school that morning). He is noticed turning around and talking to another student ("What page was that problem on?"). After three of four times of hearing his name called, the student may develop signs of paranoia. He is convinced that the teacher is picking on him. Well, is he? An examination of motives could be in order. Maybe it is just the long arm of coincidence. Perhaps the teacher is really quite unaware that he has singled him out. Perhaps not.

> Mrs. Wolfe, the typing teacher, was giving a timed speed test. She usually started each test by saying "One—Two—Three—TYPE." The students were warned not to begin typing until the word *type* had been said. Mrs. Wolfe had just said "Three" when Rosa and Phil began typing but she did not say anything. After the first test, Mrs. Wolfe told the students to get ready for a second one. Again at the count of "Three," Rosa and Phil started to type, but this time, Helen did, too. Mrs. Wolfe stopped the test and said, "Helen, you know that is cheating. Don't ever do that again." But nothing was said to Rosa or Phil. The class was convinced that Mrs. Wolfe was picking on Helen and was very unfair.

In general, nagging is particularly ineffective with boys, a point that some women teachers will never understand. Boys turn off a nagging teacher; girls are more tolerant.

How Human Can Teachers Be?

One of the most difficult things for a student to cope with is the teacher whose behavior is inconsistent; the teacher who jokes with his students one moment and then suddenly, without any warning, becomes a screaming tyrant. What should a student do? How can he be expected to play his proper role in relationship to his teacher? As a matter of fact, what is his role in such a situation? If the teacher's mood is too changeable, the student will never really know exactly what behavior in class is acceptable. How can he then comply with his teacher's wishes?

If the teacher cracks a joke about a student's behavior, perhaps saying something like this: "O.K., Marty, you've given us a good laugh. Any more?" just what is Marty to think? It would appear that his humor was appreciated by the teacher. If this is really the case, it would seem to be an open invitation for him to provide the class and the teacher with more of the same. Excessive behavior of this kind could prove disruptive to the teaching-learning situation. But does the student know this? A good laugh never hurts a class. But all students should know how much is enough. If the teacher then suddenly shouts, "Marty, stop that this minute!" Marty will probably be hurt and angry. Chances are that he was only attempting to fulfill the role which he felt was expected of him.

Students should know the teacher. His behavior should be consistent to the extent that his class knows what is expected of them and what he considers the limits of classroom propriety. If this is done, later misunderstandings of this nature will probably be avoided. If a teacher does not believe a student's behavior is appropriate, then he should leave no doubt about it in the student's mind. But the classroom tempo must be established early in the term.

Cornering

Many teachers will never be found guilty of any of the tactics cited to date. Yet despite their best efforts and intentions, on one not-so-fine day, a student replies to a teacher's statement or direction with an emphatic, "No, I won't." Just what can the teacher do at this point?

During that split second as the ominous phrase is leaving the student's lips, the teacher's mind is working (or certainly should be) with computer-like speed, deciding which of the many action options he will select. Unfortunately, to the beginning teacher there may seem only one course of action open: confrontation to force the student to bend to his will. This is one way to handle the situation, but it is only one of many possibilities and may not be the best action option to pull the teacher out of his corner (and off the spot) quickly and gracefully. Even though this approach to the problem may be selected, the teacher should also be aware of the other choices open and, what is of prime importance, the cost of selecting each.

In the first place, just what was said to bring such a response. Was it a simple direction to "open your books" or was it "Bill, go to the principal's office." The two situations obviously differ in their importance and, if the first situation resulted in a "No, I won't," it might be easier to laugh it off (the student may have just meant it facetiously) if he immediately opened his book and prepared for work. Of course, in that case, if it was said very softly so that only a few students (and unfortunately, the teacher) heard his comment, the whole thing might best be ignored.

If however, in the teacher's considered opinion, the student's behavior (or the effect of the behavior on the rest of the class) warrants some positive action on his part, he may prefer to say loud enough for the class to hear, "Bill, I want to see you at the end of class," and then continue with the lesson. Following this pattern, further discussion of the incident should await the conference with Bill at the end of the period. Nothing except the wasting of class time will be accomplished by continuing a dialogue on the matter in front of all the students. Or, if the teacher wishes to use a more mysterious approach, he can appear to ignore the remark and continue teaching the lesson. Then casually strolling down Bill's aisle, he can deposit a "see me after class" note on his desk or whisper the same message to him. In either case the lesson has been continued and the student dealt with without disrupting the class.

In the case of Bill, if his refusal was in response to the teacher's request "Go to the principal's office," it thus becomes a more serious matter than not opening his textbook when told to do so. The teacher still has several action options open to him. But selecting the inappropriate option will cause as much consternation to the teacher as to the mouse who chooses the wrong path in a maze—and frequently more trouble.

It must also be remembered that Bill is busy figuring his own action options. He may slug it out verbally with the teacher for a few minutes even though he has decided to go to the office *but under his own terms*. So he will needle the teacher just long enough to impress his audience of fellow students (his status will increase proportionately to the amount of time he can hold out) but not so long that the teacher's tolerance level is exceeded, and then stroll grandly out the door, leaving an angry teacher whose teaching will be somewhat less than inspired for the remainder of the period.

But what if Bill doesn't decide to go to the office. What if the culmination of the dialogue is his dare to "make me." Then what?

A moment or two of silence should be permitted to hang in the air. Such a silence feels as heavy and ominous as any action taken. The class will appear to hold its collective breath. The teacher might then say softly and deliberately while looking straight into the eyes of the student, "I don't think that I heard you correctly, Bill."

This is his chance. He can save a bit of "face" by muttering, "Ah, nothing" and depart to the principal's office. He at least made an attempt to prove how tough he was but at the same time he did not put himself (or his teacher, for that matter) into such a corner that the situation can only go from bad to worse. It is important at this time that the teacher not complicate the situation any more by insisting upon having the final word. Let well enough alone. Resume teaching as soon as the student has headed for the door and is on his way to the principal's office. Some teachers seem to delight in going to the classroom door with the "victim," watching as he walks down the hall, while all the time making sarcastic asides to the class.

But if Bill does not use this out, if he still refuses to leave, what then?

If the teacher is one who likes to live dangerously (remember about touching students), he can try to eject Bill physically from the classroom. He might even be successful, providing the teacher is 6 feet tall and weighs 200 pounds, depending upon Bill's size. However, this technique will have little effect if the teacher is a 95-pound (soaking wet) 5-foot female. And even if successful, such a performance lacks dignity. If the teacher is not successful, that is, if the student gets the best of him, and he finds himself in a prone position on the floor staring up at the student whom he tried to remove physically from the room, what next?

He may even find himself in real danger. In such a case, he may have to leave the room and summon aid or send a student for help. (In some schools where physical attacks upon teachers are frequent, arrangements have been worked out in advance so that teachers know how to respond to such action.)

Extreme care should be exercised whenever one attempts to use force on a student, who, however large he may be, is also a minor. Even if the teacher wins the encounter, he may lose if an irate parent brings a law suit for assault upon the person of his child. It would seem, therefore, that this action option has very little to recommend it.

The teacher is often dealing with the unknown and operating in the dark when coping with such problems. Why was the student defiant in the first place? Perhaps there could have been a valid reason, unknown to the teacher, that caused the behavior and which was totally unrelated to the classroom in which it occurred. At that moment, however, it would not appear wise to risk a further, and possibly more explosive, recital of the reasons for this student's behavior. Or is this in fact the right time or the place for a discussion of this nature, with an audience of curious students listening in?

Assuming that the action option of forcibly removing the student from the room has been rejected and talking did not accomplish the desired results either, what is left? The teacher might then say to the student, "Well, Bill, then we will have to ask Mr. Mean (the principal, naturally) to come down here, won't we?" (Again, a teacher had better be certain that whatever precipitated this situation was serious enough for this drastic action. Otherwise he may find a rather irritated principal on his hands. Or even worse, one who refuses to leave the comfort and security of his office.) The teacher can give Bill another chance by suggesting "Why don't you think about it for a minute. *You* make the decision. If you change your mind, just get up and go to the office."

The teacher then returns to the lesson or gives the other students an assignment; anything to break the tension. Also keep in mind that the incident is not closed; the students will still be watching and waiting. If Bill gets up and leaves the class, no further comment is needed. It should be remembered that the teacher is committed to this course of action. He has placed himself in the same corner that his student is in. One of the two has to give. Either the student leaves the room or the teacher must get the principal.

Beware of an action option which will force the student into the position of having to defy his teacher in order to maintain "face" with the class and with himself (a very valid motivation). To say that there is only one action option for any situation, even one of a serious nature (as mentioned above) is both false and dangerous. In our imaginary situation there were at least five possible ways of acting and reacting. We must not forget that the students also have more than one course of action open to

them in any single situation. Some teachers delude themselves
that students have but one way to react—to do what they are
told to do when they are told to do it. But this is highly unrealistic. Each day in the classroom will convince any teacher that
students can follow directions with as many variations in attitude and action as there are students under his supervision.

In situations where the student appears to be defying the
teacher, it may in reality be a case of the student defying authority.[3] Of course, there will be those times when the student is dis-
pleased with the teacher as a person. In most cases, though, he
may be reacting to a regulation or decision which runs counter
to his own wishes at that moment. Knowing and understanding
this factor may enable the teacher to retain his composure during
periods of tension and remain in complete control of the situation.

Saving Graces

Whether we can maintain classroom control depends upon how
we see ourselves—whether we are confident enough of our ability
as teachers to deal with a variety of situations objectively. Having a sense of humor will help the teacher achieve this goal. Many
teachers take themselves far too seriously. They feel that their
every utterance or action is profound and should be considered
as such by students. They are afraid to laugh, feeling that this
will breed familiarity and crack the invisible wall which separates teacher and student. Removing any barrier which prohibits
the honest exchange of ideas through teacher-student interaction
should improve, not diminish, learning and, hence, reduce problems of classroom control.

A teacher who feels secure and not threatened by his students
is able to laugh with them. Many teachers mistakenly believe
that they have this sense of humor. Too often, however, they are
laughing at students and at their mistakes. This is entirely different. When a teacher laughs at a student, it is a form of ridicule, a put down. The student feels humiliated and the atmosphere of the classroom is likely to become increasingly tense as
each student attempts to protect himself from becoming the next
target.

Of course, teachers also should be able to laugh at their own
boners. Any teacher who can appreciate the humor in his own
mistakes can lessen the distance between him and his students by

[3]Arthur L. Stinchcombe, *Rebellion in a High School* (Chicago: Quadrangle Books, Inc., 1964), pp. 15–48.

showing that he too is human, can err, and is capable of enjoying a good laugh, even at his own expense.

A teacher who knows that he can control his class is not afraid that revealing a human image will permit things to get out of hand. It is when a teacher doubts his own ability to cope with unforeseen situations that many problems may develop.

Very insecure individuals will usually choose one of two equally disastrous paths to maintain discipline in their classrooms. They will either adopt the iron fist approach, tolerating no deviation from a given order and keeping the students under control by threats and by banishments to the principal's office. Or they will be thoroughly permissive, reasoning "if the kids really like me— accept me as a pal—they will behave." Neither technique yields success in the classroom.

The teacher who resorts to temper tantrums and threats of reprisals is no model of mature, reflective behavior. Such actions are merely the defensive reactions of an individual whose self-image is so insecure that he is afraid to have the world (in the form of his students and colleagues) see him as he is (or as he sees himself). This behavior also inhibits any attempts which his students might make to know him as a person. A protective shield may also serve to stop any inroads which might expose his inadequacies and provide an excellent camouflage for a sagging ego.

On the other hand, the teacher who cajoles and pleads with his students for attention and quiet in the classroom is often merely seeking the reassurance of his own self-worth by gaining acceptance from his pupils in the form of proper behavior. He is afraid of taking a stand on a classroom issue, afraid to offend those whose support he so desperately needs. He lacks the assurance and convictions of his actions and therefore takes as little action as possible. Even when action is taken, it becomes a form of apology and a plea for forgiveness. Students do not need either type of individual as their teacher. They do need a mature adult who is fair and reasonable.

Teachers should form their own opinions about students in their classes and not prejudge them on hearsay or even from reading entries in their cumulative folders. Granted this is somewhat difficult to accomplish. Colleagues are quick to volunteer information concerning students. Usually their contributions are derogatory.

Armed with such opinions, teachers have been known to begin a school year by stating to a student: "Pete, I know *all* about you from your previous teachers. If you step out of line just *once* in my classroom, I'll have you thrown out of school." This is extremely poor judgment on the part of the teacher. Pete, like most students, probably reacts differently in each of his classes. By looking for trouble (contrary to our initial bit of advice), the teacher has already branded Pete. He has placed the student in the position of beginning a new class with two strikes against him. Calling his previous difficulties with other teachers to the student's attention has virtually closed the door to any positive behavioral change which might have occurred. Had the teacher waited to see how Pete would react in his class, his opinions could have been based on facts.

Students should be given the opportunity to establish their place in each of their five or six classes. Prejudgments based on the opinions or experiences of others deny the student an opportunity to change (if change is desirable). Very often what is expected is received. Discipline problems can be avoided by permitting every student to begin each of his classes with a clean slate. He then has a behavioral action option of his own making, not one which is influenced by the bias of his teacher.

Teachers should expect certain standards of conduct and co-operation. If it is true that man spends his entire life attempting to answer the question, "Who am I?" it is the teacher not the student, who must provide the insight. The teacher who enters the classroom seeking to find his identity at the expense of others will diminish, not strengthen, his self-image. To teach is to have direction.

Summary

The preceding pages examined how the teacher himself can unwittingly be a disturbing factor in the classroom, a catalyst that triggers unacceptable behavior by his students. The overzealous teacher, in trying to enforce each and every personal or school regulation, will soon discover that such efforts may alienate some of his students. Nevertheless each teacher must develop those behavioral and academic requirements which he feels are necessary for the teaching-learning climate of his classes.

Many classroom problems are precipitated when teachers either purposely or accidentally infringe upon the dignity of their students. This occurs in several ways—careless use of their names, confiscating students' possessions, using sarcasm or nagging, thus reducing students to a feeling of insignificance or making them mere objects of teacher hostility. All forms of physical contact between the teacher and his students need close scrutiny as to their underlying motives.

It is important that teachers develop some degree of consistent behavior within the classroom so that they do not exhibit a Dr. Jekyll and Mr. Hyde personality. Effective teachers are able to maintain open, flexible responses when dealing with disruption in the classroom. They realize the value of humor and a sense of proportion so that small situations are not magnified into major crises.

Classroom Situations

The following pages present actual situations which were either caused or further complicated by some action taken by the teacher in the classroom. When discussing the proposed options, an additional key consideration should be the recognition that there are various stages in every situation. As the issues intensify, the choice of options may narrow as the problem becomes a crisis. Several possible action options are proposed at the conclusion of each incident. Spaces have been provided following each action option for reactions, comments, and analysis. It is possible that no single action option, by itself, will solve the problem but that a combination may provide the most effective answer. Or a new option may be suggested by the reader or group.

Situation 1: "I Didn't Know You Meant It"   Mr. Jones had thought he had made the requirements for the history term paper very clear when he had discussed the dittoed sheet of directions in class several weeks earlier. Each student was to submit his paper in a three-hole theme binder with all bibliographic references written on 4 x 6-inch cards clipped to the first page of the report.

Collecting the papers, he reached the last desk in the last row. Mary Ellis handed him a manila file folder containing two-hole paper with 3 x 5-inch reference cards attached.

"Mary, what is the meaning of this?" Mr. Jones asked.

"What do you mean, Mr. Jones?"

"You know very well what I mean, young lady. It is obvious that you have not met the requirements I established for this paper. It is not in a binder, the paper is wrong, and so are your reference cards."

"Does that really matter. I did the work. Besides, I used the things we had at home," Mary replied.

"It matters, Mary. I will only accept work that is correct."

"But it is correct. I spent *hours* in that dumb library looking all of this up. If you don't look at it, how will you know whether it is correct or not?"

An agitated Mr. Jones responded, "Mary, why do you think that you should be the only student in the class who does not need to comply with simple instruction?"

"I just didn't think that paper and cards and cover were *that* important. I thought that you were more interested in what I wrote. You never really said that you wouldn't accept a different kind of paper and cards. I'm sorry; I just didn't understand. Please take my paper; I worked so hard on it!"

Mr. Jones . . .

Action Options

1. . . . accepts the paper but informs Mary publicly that her grade will be lowered for failing to comply with the requirements.

2. ... refuses to accept the paper until it is submitted in the proper form.

3. ... accepts the paper without further comment and does not penalize Mary for not following directions since she didn't understand their importance.

4. ... accepts the paper to determine its quality before deciding to have it redone or to lower Mary's grade.

5. . . . asks Mary to come by after school to discuss the matter further.

6. . . . explains to Mary and the entire class once again the reasons for requiring a certain format.

7. . . . (your solution)

Situation 2: "Keep Your Distance." Mr. Younger, a math teacher, felt that his classes would be more efficient if they were operated on a no-nonsense, impersonal, business-like basis. To facilitate this approach, he decided to call all students by their last names. One day after he had written a problem on the board, he turned to one of the students and asked, "Harper, how would you solve for x in this case?" There was no response. "Harper, didn't you hear me? I asked how you would find x in this equation?"

The boy looked at the problem, then at the teacher. "I heard you, *Younger*," he responded.

"That's *Mr.* Younger," his teacher answered.

"How come *you* can call everybody in here by their last names but we have to say Mister to you? My name is Jim; everyone else calls me that—friends, teachers, everyone but *you*. I don't like being called *Harper*. It makes me feel like a "nothing." If you want me to answer any more of your questions, you'll have to call me Jim like everyone else."

There was a loud muttering of agreement from the other students.

Mr. Younger looked at Jim and the rest of the class and . . .

Action Options

1. . . . demanded an apology from Jim before resuming.

2. . . . apologized to the class for unintentionally offending them.

3. . . . reminded the class that the teacher makes the rules and calls the shots.

4. . . . sent Jim to the office for deliberate rudeness.

5. . . . explained to the class why he used only last names.

Situation 3. "Operation—Radio Removal"   The day that Mrs. Blackwell began her unit on Stephen Crane's *Red Badge of Courage* just happened to be the opening day of the baseball season. Prior to reading the novel, she was lecturing about the author's life and the conditions in the United States immediately preceding the Civil War, the period in which the novel is set. Suddenly, the unmistakable sounds of a radio could be heard in the room. She stopped and looked around but the sound had ceased, so she resumed teaching. Once again a faint voice could be heard announcing the starting lineups. Again she looked around the room attempting to locate the radio. Once again, the sound stopped.

Resuming her lecture, Mrs. Blackwell began to walk slowly around the room. She reached Dick Robert's desk just in time to hear "Play ball!" The radio was camouflaged behind Dick's notebook.

"I'll take that," she said holding out her hand.

Dick turned the radio off. "I'm sorry. I'll put it away right now."

"I said give me that radio immediately."

"I put it away and apologized. What more do you want?"

"I want the radio, *now*. I don't intend to discuss it any further. Hand it over."

"Look, Mrs. Blackwell," Dick pleaded, "it isn't my radio. It belongs to my father and he doesn't even know that I took it. He's going to be awfully mad if anything happens to it. It cost $50. Please!"

"You should have thought about that before bringing it to class. I've wasted enough time on you. Hand it over. You'll get it back at the end of the week."

Dick was obviously weighing his dilemma. An angry father or teacher, either way he lost. Finally he said very quietly, "No, Mrs. Blackwell, I'm sorry but I can't give it to you."

Mrs. Blackwell then decided to . . .

Action Options

1. . . . forcibly take the radio from Dick.

2. . . . permit Dick to keep the radio since he promised not to play it in class.

3. . . . send Dick to the office with a note explaining the situation and his defiance.

4. . . . send a note to Dick's father explaining his son's behavior and the fact that he had "borrowed" the radio.

5. . . . ask the class if they would like to hear some of the game and do their work at home.

6. . . . (your solution)

Situation 4: "Let Go!"   For weeks Eddie had been "smart mouthing" Mr. Bosley in class. Anything that Mr. Bosley said or did brought some wise response from Eddie. The teacher had tried talking to Eddie after class but had accomplished nothing. For some unknown reason, Eddie had an intense dislike for Mr. Bosley which he delighted in expressing loudly and frequently.

After Mr. Bosley had announced a test for the following week, Eddie called out, "Oh, another Bosley bomb!" Mr. Bosley marched back to Eddie's desk and grabbed the boy by the shoulder pulling him to his feet. "Let's go, wise guy. The principal is going to have to deal with you. I have had it!"

Eddie was half walking and being half dragged toward the classroom door by Mr. Bosley, "God dammit, let go! I can walk by myself!"

"What did you say, young man?" demanded the teacher.

"You heard me. I can walk by myself."

"That's not what you said, but you'll walk the way *I* want you to walk!"

Eddie stopped and attempted to pull his arm free. "Take your damn hands off of me you bastard, or so help me God, I'll punch you right in the mouth."

Mr. Bosley released his arm and . . .

Action Options

1. . . . decided to settle the matter once and for all by telling Eddie to make his play.

2. . . . allowed Eddie to walk to the principal's office under his own power.

3.   ... apologized for using force and sent Eddie to the office with a note explaining his behavior.

4.   ... explained to Eddie that teachers have certain rights and that he will be in serious difficulties should he strike a teacher.

5.   ... (your solution)

Situation 5: "Who's The Expert?" A discussion of the accomplishments of Franklin D. Roosevelt's administration was underway in the government class. Mrs. Jackson, the teacher, had stated that "Roosevelt saved the nation from extinction in the '30s. Without his firm handling of the nation's problems, there could have been anarchy. He was one of the greatest of our presidents."

Joe Adams raised his hand. "Mrs. Jackson, how can you say that Roosevelt was great when he did so many things which were later ruled unconstitutional?"

"Why, Joe, I didn't know that you were a legal expert. Please enlighten us a little further on the subject."

"Ah, well," Joe stammered, "he made businessmen agree to take only a certain profit and things like that, didn't he? That sounds like what the communists do."

"Oh, really?" answered Mrs. Jackson. "Are you claiming that Roosevelt was a communist? I didn't realize that you were also an expert on economics."

Joe is becoming defensive. "I only meant how can what Roosevelt did be so great when it wasn't democratic?"

"Do you deny, Joe, that the nation began to recover after his policies were put into effect? Do you?"

"Well, I suppose so, but isn't that the same as saying that the end justifies the means?"

Mrs. Jackson loses her composure at this point. "That does it! Now you want to debate ethics. Joe, you amaze me. Your knowledge runs the gamut from constitutional expert and defender of democracy to moralist. I think that you have contributed enough for today."

Blushing, Joe blurts, "I don't claim to be any of those things. You ask for our opinions but if they don't agree with yours, you smash us. All you want us to do is agree with you."

At this point, it is obvious that Mrs. Jackson should . . .

Action Options

    1. . . . demand an immediate apology from Joe and close the incident.

2. ... request that Joe return after school for a further discussion of the matter.

3. ... pause for a moment and reconsider the preceding events before determining if an apology is in order, and if it is, from whom.

4. ... ask Joe for an explanation of his last remark and open the situation to total class discussion.

Situation 6: "Tell Me!"   Mr. Franklin began his geography class by asking his students to tell what thoughts, words, or phrases came to mind when they heard the word *Bagdad*. His intention was to motivate thinking on the topic. The students were responding well when he noticed Bill turn around and say something to the boys seated behind him. Bill's comment brought peals of laughter from them, and the entire class looked in their direction.

"What did you say, Bill?" Mr. Franklin asked, walking down the aisle and stopping by Bill's desk.

"It was nothing," came the reply.

"It *must* have been something because people don't laugh about nothing. Tell us; we could use some humor at this point."

"Really, it wasn't funny. Those guys would laugh at anything."

"Bill, I *insist* that you repeat exactly what you said."

Bill shrugged his shoulders. "Okay, but remember I didn't want to. All I said was, 'ain't it a damn shame that we don't have a deluxe model Bagdad carpet to fly us out of this stupid class.' "

The class howled and Mr. Franklin . . .

Action Options

1. . . . ignored Bill's remarks and resumed the class.

2. . . . informed Bill that if he spent less time being humorous and more time listening that he might do better work.

Suggested Readings

Bandura, Albert. *Principles of Behavior Modification*. New York: Holt, Rinehart & Winston, Inc., 1969. A thorough, clear, presentation of the basic psychological principles governing human behavior within the conceptual framework of social learning with many implications for the classroom teacher.

Clark, Leonard H., ed. *Strategies and Tactics in Secondary School Teaching: A Book of Readings*. New York: The Macmillan Company, 1968. Chap. 6. Six articles discussing the changing nature of discipline in secondary schools and the techniaues holding most promise for success.

LaGrand, Louis E. *Discipline in the Secondary School*. West Nyack, N.Y.: Parker Publishing Co., 1969. Deals with various types of student problems and how the teacher can cope with them.

National Commission of Teacher Education and Professional Standards. *The Real World of the Teacher*. Report of the 19th National T.E.P.S. Conference. Washington, D.C.: National Education Association, 1965. Explores the problems facing beginning teachers in their formative years.

Skinner, B. F. *The Technology of Teaching*. New York: Appleton-Century-Crofts, 1968. Chap. 9. Traces the causes of discipline problems, the effects and limitations of punishment and techniques designed to change attitudes using respondent behavior.

Wittenberg, Rudolph M. *Discipline in the Teens*. New York: Association Press, 1963. Discussion of the basic ways of dealing with adolescents.

3

Student-Caused Problems

In the previous chapter, we developed the idea that at times it is actually the teacher who causes some of the discipline problems within his classroom. But it should also be remembered that when a problem develops, more than one person is usually involved. Of course, we are referring to the well-known fact that by their attitudes or actions students, as well as teachers, may be the originators of classroom problems.

This chapter will focus on classroom situations in which the pupil assumes the aggressive role and initiates the disorder. He has, in effect, taken the play away from the teacher and the lesson, moving the center of classroom attention to himself. The teacher must reverse this momentum and return class attention to relevant academic matters.

The introductory chapter of this book asked whether something had happened to our adolescents. What has changed them in recent years from relatively sweet, reasonable, and cooperative creatures into sometimes frighteningly sophisticated young adults whose attitudes towards school, education, teachers—in fact toward all forms of duly constituted authority—appear at times unreasonable, unpredictable, and often explosive?

With this question in mind, perhaps what is needed is a closer look at today's adolescents,[1] their motives for being in school, their diverse needs, and the complex array of problems which accompanies them from class to class.

Many youths are fighting desperately to achieve some sense of identity and self-worth in this age of the computer and mass education. Some of our schools frequently appear to exert little, if any, effort to make young people feel particularly welcome or even comfortable within the educational atmosphere. Students feel harassed by rules which seem puzzling, whimsical, bewildering, frustrating, and out of date.

Some youths recede in lonely isolation from other students and from the adult world. This is a withdrawal from a reality which is too painful to resist but, at the same time, too harsh to accept, and too complex to cope with. Often teachers incorrectly identify this reaction as a lack of motivation on the part of the student. Or, even worse, they insinuate that many youth are uneducable because of their apparent hostility or sullenness; such students could not possibly want to learn! Yet this facade may in reality be an expression of the rejection[2] which these youths feel toward a system which, to them, hampers their freedom, dictates how they will spend every minute of five or six precious hours of each day, bores them with material that many teachers admit has little bearing on contemporary life, and then finally acknowledges their efforts to conform by labeling them failures.

How can we honestly expect a student to believe that we consider him an important, worthwhile individual if we consistently (and often with due deliberation) make it impossible for him to achieve success? In the mind of the student, teachers are constantly laying traps for him with their myriad rules, waiting for him to slip from grace so that he can be caught. It appears to be a sadistic game that teachers play at the expense of their students. As a further irritant, failure is dispensed in two forms—informal and formal. For reasons known only to themselves, some

[1]For a thorough examination of the development of the individual and effect on behavior, see Anne Anastasi, *Differential Psychology: Individual and Group Differences in Behavior* (New York: The Macmillan Company, 1958), Theodore Lidz, *The Person: His Development Through the Life Cycle* (New York: Basic Books, Inc., Publishers, 1968.)

[2]For an interesting report on research into the causes of rebellion in high schools and the characteristics of school rebels, suggesting the causes of rebellion stem from alienation from the school's status systems, see Arthur L. Stinchcombe, *Rebellion in a High School* (Chicago: Quadrangle Books, Inc., 1964).

teachers informally brand a student a failure by their tone of voice or choice of words when the student does not respond as expected. Then the formal pronouncement may be made with a big, bold *F* placed clearly on the report card which, in turn, must be carried home and presented to the parents for their signature (acknowledgment). Even systems which do not require cards to be signed and returned really offer no relief. The failure is still duly and publicly noted.

What should the student expect from his parents when this formal declaration of academic defeat is placed in their hands? Sympathy and understanding? Such a reaction is possible, but it is highly improbable. Too many parents see a failing grade on their child's report card as the school's indictment not only of their child's ability but a reflection on them as parents. Hence, when the child fails, it is the failure of the parents. They react, in turn, by berating their child for his ingratitude (for all they have done for him), his lack of diligence ("your *father* never failed"), and his unresponsive attitude ("you just don't give a damn, do you?"). As a final blow, they sometimes suspend all of his so-called privileges (those little things which help him exist as a teenager—dates, use of the car, and his allowance).

Or like Pontius Pilate, they may wash their hands of the entire affair. "It's your *F*, Bill; *you* do something about it. After all, school is *your* job, not mine." Punishment is bad enough. However, parental indifference, like teacher indifference, will almost compel the student to choose a behavior which will force someone who matters to take notice. He *will* get recognition, even if it is not of the most pleasant form.

It would appear difficult for a youth to establish and maintain good rapport with a teacher who considers him a failure. As far as the student is concerned, the teacher is saying, "You're worthless, kid; you're not too quick." Day after day, year after year, some students receive nothing but below average or failing grades. They may be promoted and nominally kept with their age group, but in the classroom they feel lost, even unable to survive in an alien world. Is it any wonder then that many decide to gain status in the only way which is available to them— through defiance, disobedience, disorder, psychotic withdrawal, or dropping out? The logic, if it can be termed that, is of a defeatist nature: "If I can't be one of the smartest kids in the school, then I'll be the worst kid in the school." As the noted psychiatrist, Dr. William Glasser, author of the book *Reality Therapy*, has said, these youngsters are the lonely failures who live in isolation and segregation, fighting the world and breaking the rules or withdrawing—checking out. They vandalize and destroy the institution which appears callously to reject them because in their frustration and pain, they can see no place to go. What other course is open to them?

Even if a student is not experiencing academic difficulty in school, he may be still the victim of many more pressures than most adults care to admit. The drive to get into college—the right college, of course—can begin as early as kindergarten in some of the more "progressive" communities. By the time that the youngster reaches junior high school, he has been thoroughly convinced that if one is to make it in our society, he must have a good education. In this sense, a good education means following the rules, mastering the curricula, and making good grades.

This in itself is a frustrating thought. The knowledge explosion (with knowledge doubling every decade) presents a voracious monster becoming more demanding each year. In effect, one is learning for obsolescence. This is what the student faces as he approaches the first hurdle, his high school diploma. Once he achieves this goal, he will then be permitted to strive for the bachelor's degree and then advanced degrees and so on until he withdraws from the intellectual arena or dies.

Those not so academically talented or interested, who feel that the maximum educational commitment they can make is for twelve years, may begin to look upon the school, as the years slowly drag by, as a prison so oppressive at times that they want to break out. This they do in the only way available to them, by causing some type of classroom crisis. Their actions may simply be a form of meaningless protest against the futility or the inevitability of an education which they do not see as either relevant or important in terms of their life goals.

Furthermore, in our fast-paced society the inducements and pressures[3] exerted by his peers to try various things for kicks—drugs, booze, sex—compounded by the general air of permissiveness in many homes today place a heavy burden on the youngster to form moral judgments which he may feel ill-equipped to make. Added to all these pressures are the usual stresses and conflicts which accompany puberty. As a result the adolescent emerges as an immature individual (part child, seeking to be protected, cared for, and accepted, and part adult, seeking independence,

[3]S. L. Halleck, M.D., "Hypotheses of Student Unrest," *Phi Delta Kappan* 50, No. 1 (September, 1968) : 2–9.

adventure, and status) caught between a series of equally strong and compelling forces.

It should quickly be noted, of course, that many of the students are neither so beset nor beseiged by the problems of maturation that they are incapable of enjoying life most of the time. The actual number who are withdrawing—mentally tuning out of class—because of their inability or desire to change what they consider their "failure identity"[4] is unknown. One might suspect, however, that the percentage is higher than most teachers would care to believe. At the same time it should be remembered that most carefree, happy, well-adjusted teenagers will at some time or other display all the melancholy of the tragic Dane. Teachers, as mature adults with admirable self-control, should be able to compensate for their students' somewhat irrational and erratic transgressions and not turn a trivial incident into a federal case.

Yet the beginning teacher, only a few years away from high school, is himself not finished growing up. Without experience to draw upon, he may lack the perceptiveness to see classroom problems in an accurate perspective and may permit small situations to develop into crises.

It would be almost impossible to guess which student will cause what type of disciplinary problem in any given classroom at any given moment on any given day. Usually more than one factor is involved when trouble occurs. No one can tell who will emerge as the villain or victim. The most retiring student in class may be the one who suddenly exhibits an uncontrollable temper or an inclination toward hysteria. On a lesser scale, a normally well-behaved youngster may drive his teacher up the wall by unconsciously humming his favorite recording group's latest hit during the entire period.

The inexperienced teacher may look upon any interruption in class as deviant behavior. The very bright student and the lonely adolescent seeking attention who often call out answers may prove so irritating that they become discipline problems in the mind of the teacher. Then there are those students whose behavior indicates emotional disturbance; their outbursts are probably not directed at the teacher personally, yet how can the teacher respond appropriately if he misunderstands their actions?

The student who disagrees or challenges the teacher may be reflecting the age of dissent in which he lives, in which many

[4]For an approach to the solution of the problem see William Glasser, M.D., *Schools Without Failure* (New York: Harper & Row, Publishers, 1969).

previously accepted absolutes are questioned. Yet such behavior is labeled deviant by the teacher who is unable to see that such a difference of opinion may be the student's attempt at independent thinking.

Irritations

Perhaps the most difficult thing for the student to learn is, in today's jargon, to "keep his cool" and when he is still angry with Teacher B in his preceding class (or his girl friend, or his parents, or life for that matter), not to release his frustrations through unacceptable behavior on unsuspecting, innocent, Teacher C. Because they are still relatively immature, students frequently find themselves incapable or unwilling to control their anger or readjust their perspectives. They cannot forget about Teacher B's class (or their other problems). Instead, this package of frustration or rage comes into the classroom, sits down, and like a lighted fuse waits for the teacher to make just one wrong move which will press the trigger to release these pent-up emotions in one glorious explosion. The teacher who enjoys good rapport with his students will be quick to notice when a student seems upset or angry and will not thoughtlessly provoke a situation by badgering the youngster for his apparent inattention.

Of course, it is true that for some students irritating the teacher is their favorite indoor school sport. They are masters at this game, and one might suspect that they helped to write the rule book. They have had no traumatic experience with another teacher before entering the room; their girl friend loves them (only God knows why!) ; and they have arrived at their own form of peace with the world. To them, teacher-baiting is a cheap and challenging form of entertainment to occupy an otherwise dull day. It is sometimes an unpleasant awakening for teachers to recognize the cold, hard facts that there are many youngsters in their classes who do not wish to be in school at all; who find any aspect of the curriculum offered to them totally boring and irrelevant, and any discipline oppressive. Yet the teacher cannot ignore these students. Whether by law or parental edict, they *are* in school, and they may be resolved to make life "interesting" for the teacher as often as possible.

A student need not cause a major disruption in class to reach some teachers. There are little annoyances which will drive a teacher with a low tolerance level batty if administered in heavy doses or over an extended period of time. An example of this is foot-tapping. Many a student taps his foot on the floor because of nervousness, excitement, or to get the teacher's goat. One foot tapping is not such a big thing. Yet as an accompaniment to teaching a class, it can become extremely annoying. Very often a look at the offending student will be all that is necessary to quell the tap, tap, tap.

Another example is the general, hopefully friendly, roughhousing which follows younger secondary male students from the halls and into the classroom. If this is continued after the bell has sounded, it will become almost impossible to begin a class. The problem with this type of activity is that it may often lead to more aggressive feelings (or may be based on real hostility). A simple statement that physical activities should be confined to the gym may be adequate to remind the students involved that the classroom is not the place for roughhousing.

Continual Yaking (Don't they ever run down?)   One of those little things which gnaws away at the teacher's nerves is a couple of perpetual talkers in his class. Frequently of the female gender, they arrive at the classroom with mouths running in high gear, talking, talking, talking. By a cruel twist of fate, these two have been deprived of each other's company for the previous period, so the amount of vital news which must be exchanged is staggering. Quick action is called for. As the words fly, the girls indicate their complete understanding through a series of squeals and giggles (at least until the bell for class rings). Once class has officially begun, the conversation hopefully will be redirected through teacher-student interaction.

If not, a significant glance directed at the dynamic duo may quell them momentarily. As soon as the teacher turns his head, they go at it again with renewed vigor. The teacher may then ask them, in a somewhat strained tone of voice, to "please stop the talking." The second request for a discontinuance of the conversation (the initial request being complied with for two minutes or less) is usually delivered in an acid tone and a glare which would melt steel. But our heroines are not to be deterred. News is news and it must be disseminated. The teacher may accompany this third request with a statement that if the conversation is so interesting, the girls may go out in the hall and *finish* it, or just plain *go*! Since the conversation is obviously important to the girls, the teacher could provide them with an opportunity to complete it without any penalty should they decide to leave the room.

Other teachers employ the silent treatment. They simply stop teaching, look pointedly at the two, and wait. The ensuing silence usually causes the talkers to halt momentarily and look up to see what has happened. Students have accused such teachers of utilizing the evil eye against them, but this charge has never been substantiated.

Now Hear This (Even if you don't want to)   Constantly calling out in class may annoy teacher and students alike when others are speaking or attempting to speak. There are students who consider this type of interruption as a very effective means of halting class productivity. No matter what the teacher says or does, Herbie blurts out an answer or poses a question. This is usually accompanied by a broad smile directed to his approving constituents. Herbie is a polite student and feigns an honest interest and concern about what is going on in class. It would indeed be a heartless teacher who would call such a student a troublemaker. It is quite possible his object is not to make trouble; he may be a bright student bored by the slowness of the class. Yet, if such outbursts are permitted to continue, the amount of work covered will decrease considerably. Hints often fall on deaf ears. Herbie is seeking attention, perhaps even approval, from the teacher (which is a basic need of us all). Nothing short of a shot between the eyes will fell him. In this case, it is best to have a private talk with him. Is he really interested or merely playing the big shot? Once this has been determined, the teacher can then decide how to proceed.

Sassing (The smart mouth)   Perhaps the most irritating type of student any teacher encounters is the smart mouth. This gem of an individual comes in both sexes and is commonly found attempting to put down the teacher or his fellow students. No matter what the teacher says or does, he is subjected to some smart remark. After a while (especially if the teacher has mouthly students in each of his classes), he begins to believe that someone up there does not like him. He may even dread the arrival of a particular class each day.

Ignoring such a student often works because he has not gotten the expected response from the teacher and, therefore, may discontinue his activities. However, if this fails, the best approach is to have a talk with the student in private and attempt to discover what motivates him to react in such a way. If this does not work, the teacher may have to resort to letting the student and class know that such behavior is unacceptable by using a firm but pointed tone of voice.

Rod was constantly making wise remarks in psychology class. He was a very good student and considered himself the class wit. Although his teacher, Mr. Otis, recognized that Rod was attempting to fill this role, his disruptions were becoming too frequent. After several talks with Rod had failed to produce the desired results, Mr. Otis took direct action. The next time Rod made some smart comment about another student's contribution, Mr. Otis said quietly, "Rod, please confine your comments to the topic under discussion."

Sarcasm should not enter into the picture since it is a negative form of criticism and provides no basis for the student's future growth.

If all else fails, a visit to the administrator's office may be in order since it is here that the power of banishment resides. While a smart mouth student may not be malicious in his remarks, his constant interruptions must be stopped for effective learning to take place.

Love (Who is your true love . . . this week?)   To consider a more pleasant type of problem we will briefly look at the phenomenon known as love, sometimes called a crush, or a case of hot-bloodedness. This occurs in two forms, both of which could disrupt the classroom. The first form, student to student, is highly natural in the adolescent and even desirable. However, for the teacher attempting to conduct a class, a couple in the back of the room holding hands or engaging in some light necking could present a problem. The two students involved will be oblivious to what the teacher is attempting to do; other students may find the performance fascinating to watch.

Just calling the students by name may break the spell and bring their attention back to the class. They may continue to spend their time looking dreamily at each other but at least this is a less distracting activity. Such behavior is perfectly natural in the adolescent, and teachers should not become overly concerned unless their actions are distracting to the other students.

The second form of classroom love is the crush that a student may get on his instructor. Many adolescents beguiled by TV and movies feel that it is absolutely imperative to be in love a good portion of the time. As they look around for a likely candidate, their attention may settle on the handsome new math teacher or the attractive English teacher if someone nearer their own age is not available. Older than their immediate peers (ah, but not too old!), the teacher suddenly becomes the epitome of the beautiful, the learned, and, depending upon the teacher's personality, the sophisticated, witty, and worldly. It is highly flattering to be held in such esteem and perhaps a bit too ego-inflating for some teachers who seem thoroughly to enjoy such childish adulation. Yet, the seeds of a dangerous situation may exist. Sometimes the teacher is not immediately aware of the crush and his (or her) efforts to be pleasant to the student (to all students, naturally) are misconstrued as proof positive that the feeling is reciprocated.

It usually becomes evident that the student's interest in the subject matter causing the sudden need for additional assistance day after day is not as academic as the teacher first thought. Once the attention is understood, the teacher should do everything in his power to discourage the student without embarrassment. The teacher should also avoid any isolated conference with the student. Unfortunately, some students have extremely vivid imaginations and can dramatize an innocent meeting into a highly compromising situation. Usually the infatuation (like student to student infatuations) dies a natural death in a short period of time. Until then, the teacher must be extremely alert to understand the dynamics of the situation. The student who feels spurned, rejected, or angry with her idol can insinuate improper conduct by the instructor or can be pushed out of contact with others forever. Furthermore, the teacher does not want to destroy rapport with the student. A little sensitivity on the part of the teacher can eliminate any significant problems.[5]

Meeting Responsibilities

One of the quickest ways a student can irritate his teacher is by failing to meet his responsibilities. Just as the teacher has certain responsibilities within the classroom, so does the student. When either teacher or student neglects these obligations, then trouble is likely to occur. Students are very quick to identify duties which are exclusively the responsibility of the teacher and become highly critical if they are not met. On the other hand, they tend to be rather blasé when it comes to their own obligations and responsi-

[5]Sidney Berman, et al., "Crushes: What Should You Do About Them," *Today's Education* 58, No. 9 (December, 1969): 12–16.

bilities to the class—unless they have accepted them as worthwhile activities.

Tardiness (Drop in any time)   Many teachers find that the student who seems perpetually late for class provides one of their most perplexing problems. There are certainly times when students have valid reasons for tardiness and the teacher will accept them. It is the perennially tardy student with no reasonable excuse for his lateness who is likely to annoy the teacher. With uncanny ability, such a student manages to time his arrival to coincide exactly with the moment when the teacher is driving home or summarizing a particular point. Just at that magical moment, when the teacher finally has gained the undivided attention of the entire class, the door is thrown open with the force of a bulldozer and in saunters Ted Tardy, the persistently late arriver. Employing all the wiles and blandishments of a con man, Ted inevitably has secured an Excused Late Admit slip from the office. Now Ted knows by this time that the very sight of the excuse will raise his teacher's blood pressure by at least ten points, but that is part of the game. After placing the slip on the desk and flashing his winning smile, he lazily strolls to his seat while acknowledging the grins of all his fans on both sides of the aisle.

The teacher should be very careful in a situation like this. Once the office has officially excused a student's tardiness by giving him an admit slip, the teacher is likely to feel trapped and outmaneuvered since he is forced to admit him, even if he does not consider the excuse reasonable. An occasional tardiness is understandable. Unfortunately, when this type of behavior becomes chronic, the parent may be an ally of the youth by providing him with the necessary written alibi or reason. Then the problem becomes multidimensional—it no longer has a single focus after the parents enter the picture. (This aspect will be explored in more detail in Chapter Five, Parent-Caused Problems.)

In most schools, there are two types of late admit slips. The first type is used only to admit the student to school after attendance has been taken to determine who is absent for the day. After that, once he has officially (as far as the office is concerned) arrived on the premises and been duly counted by his homeroom teacher, the bell announcing the beginning and ending of each class becomes the final arbiter of lateness.

It is in this area that some students will occasionally try the limits of a teacher's patience by attempting to gain a few additional minutes with a buddy or girl friend in the hall while the bell is in the actual process of ringing and then make a mad dash for their seats. No wise teacher sends a student to the office for an infraction of this nature. Experience has indicated that the office will send the student directly back to his classroom. Why? Actually, it is quite simple. The office has neither the desire nor inclination (nor staff) to babysit any teacher's students. There are far more pressing problems awaiting their attention. This is one issue which the teacher and student must settle for themselves.

Besides, what is late? This is something which the teacher should have clearly defined at the beginning of the school year. The student should know whether being on time means one toe in the door when the bell stops ringing, or if he must already be in his seat, ready for action. Unless the teacher has been very clear about this requirement, the student will attempt to forestall the inevitable beginning of class for as long as possible, especially if the class is dull, the teacher primitive, and if failure or ridicule await him.

Frequently a student is late and has a very good reason. Sometimes he will be detained by another teacher. Or he may have been detained in the office on official business. When the student comes into the classroom after the class has begun, he should know what is expected. If school policy requires a written excuse, this should be placed on the teacher's desk, and the student should take his seat with as little disruption of the class as possible. Otherwise, an oral explanation at the end of the class will suffice.

But what if, in the teacher's mind, the student is late for no reason? Lateness in such a situation is likely to produce a defensive student. He knows that he has had it (or is going to get it). Under such circumstances, reasons the student, the best defense is a strong offense. Unless the teacher is extremely careful, valuable class time will be wasted in meaningless dialogue with the student on why he wasn't here when he should have been. Sometimes, upon entering the classroom, he may interrupt the teacher with a "You'll never believe this, but I was late because my coat got stuck in the locker and I couldn't get free." The experienced teacher will never permit the student to advance beyond "You'll never believe this . . ." before immediately redirecting the attention of the class (which is now waiting to hear a good excuse for their own future use) by saying, "Well, maybe I will, Dick, but we will talk about it in private after class. Now, please take your seat." (It is not a question of doubting the student but of the appropriate time and place to discuss a personal matter.)

The discussion is ended when the teacher returns his full attention to the class and resumes teaching. A student is not likely to continue a conversation with someone who has stopped listening and is ignoring his very existence. The student's only practical option (short of leaving the classroom) is to go to his seat. This is precisely what the teacher wanted.

Some teachers fall into the trap carefully laid by students of debating the whys and wherefores of the tardiness with the student before the entire class. Any good strategist should know that one never fights a battle on his opponent's ground and under his terms. The clever fighter always chooses the time, place, and conditions that are most advantageous to him.

Once the class has ended, both teacher and student can quietly, and without an audience, discuss the merits of his case, determining whether there were extenuating circumstances. Obviously, it is ridiculous to make an issue over a one-in-a-lifetime offense. Simply ignore it. Of course, if the student missed important material, arrangements will have to be worked out for his making it up. This should be accomplished at the teacher's convenience (after all, it was the student who was late).

Absenteeism (Now you see them; now you don't)   Although there are times when a teacher may send up a prayer of thanks because a certain troublesome student is absent, it may not be such a blessing after all. After a few days' absence, he will feel lost and unable to follow the class. Often discovering how much work he has missed (and must make up) adds to his feeling of being completely out of it. Should the teacher call upon him too soon after his return, he may accusingly remind him, "I was absent last week; how should *I* know what is going on?" (Such a statement probably would irritate his teacher and could lead to a fruitless dialogue between them.) Inability to follow the material under consideration will heighten his frustration concerning the amount of work missed. Or the student may become so bored that he seeks some other form of diversion during the period such as talking to his neighbor, passing notes, putting his head down on the desk and pretending to sleep, jabbing someone with a pencil, kicking his shoe (or someone else's) down the aisle. These measures may not be deliberately designed to prevent the teacher from advancing into new material but chances are that they will prove effective delaying tactics. And, although the student's motives may simply be trying not to fall any farther behind in his work, his behavior could force the teacher to censure him publicly; thus adding further to his feeling unwanted and unaccepted.

At the beginning of the school year the teacher and his students together should determine a procedure to deal with returning absentees. A student would not then return to the classroom after some days' absence feeling that he is about to be buried alive. He would trust the teacher to provide some way for him to catch up. If he has been absent for some time and (in the opinion of both teacher and student) will not be able to profit from the class because he has missed important background material, it might be wisest and kindest to send him to the library with a specific assignment. Or, perhaps another student could accompany him to a quiet corner somewhere in the school (although due to crowded conditions in many schools it may be difficult to find one) to acquaint him with the work missed. The returning student should also be helped to arrange a conference with his teacher immediately so that definite plans can be made to bring him back into the mainstream of things as quickly and painlessly as possible.

Most student illnesses are quite genuine. However, there are times when because of pressures, real or imagined, exerted upon them, students choose to become ill rather than to face their school responsibilities. For example, a few students follow a pattern of missing school on the day of a big test or the day that term papers are due. They return the following day and are prepared to take a makeup test or submit the work. They usually have a note signed by their parents. After this has happened several times, it will become obvious that the teacher must work with both the student and parents to determine whether a real problem exists or if the student is playing some kind of game. Most of the time, parents are unaware of the various games their children play concerning school. Unfortunately, it is sometimes true that parents are fully aware of these antics and lend their support and cooperation. (This aspect of the absence problem will be explored again in a later chapter on parent-caused problems.)

Homework (How not to spend an evening)   Each student has certain class responsibilities which must be met. These may include completing homework assignments, taking tests, making up work when absent, and participating in class discussions and activities. These requirements vary from teacher to teacher and subject to subject. The working framework for the course should be clearly stated at the beginning of the school year. This does not eliminate flexibility but merely gives the students some idea of the extent of their obligations. As the course evolves, various changes may be necessary to meet newly recognized needs and interests. However, at all times students should know what is expected of them and be given sufficient time to meet these expectations. Most students will meet most of their obligations most of the time (just as their adult models fulfill most of their responsibilities most of the time!).

The beginning teacher mistakenly believes that he can make his students do what he feels is necessary for their educational growth. It is often with a sinking heart and bruised ego that he learns that a teacher really cannot make his student do anything unless the student really wants to do so.

Homework, for instance, has at times proved to be the Waterloo from which some teachers have not returned. Many youths (top students as well as failing ones) pride themselves on never taking a book home and never, no, never, doing any homework. We could debate the pedagogic benefits of any homework assignment that students find repugnant—but we won't. Everyone at one time or another has been assigned homework which by the very mildest of descriptions could be termed busy work. Students have coined even more graphic words to describe such work. (They are *tired* at the end of a long school day, which may total 10 to 12 hours, counting travel, school, and homework time.)

The teacher believes he *has* assigned work which is relevant in terms of students' needs and interests, which will require a reasonable amount of time to complete, and which has been geared to the various ability levels of the class. Granted this would take considerably more effort on the teacher's part than just saying, as the bell is ringing at the end of the period, "Oh, class, read pages 282 through 294 and answer the questions at the end of the chapter for tomorrow." If we accept the premise that the homework meets these criteria, we will still be faced with students who simply will not do it.

Anne was a very bright student who never did homework for any of her classes. Before the first marking period, her math, world history, and German teachers discussed her work with her in their respective classes. Mr. Morelli, the math teacher, told her, "Anne, you never turned in any of the assigned homework, but you always get *A* on the tests, so it's obvious you didn't need to do it." Mrs. Henson, the world history teacher, said to her, "Anne you always get *A* on your tests but you have refused to color in the maps required, so I'm going to lower your grade." Miss Terry, the German teacher, while admitting that Anne had a straight *A* average on all the tests given to date added, "Anne, homework is a required part of this course; unless you submit it before the end of the grading period, your mark will suffer."

Before determining which course he will follow, the teacher should reexamine the purpose and validity of the homework as well as what was said to the students at the beginning of the school year concerning the weight given to homework in the final grade, and whether students achieving a certain average would be exempt from doing it. The wise teacher announces the rules at the outset and thus avoids getting himself trapped by such a situation at the end of the grading period.

But what about the student who doesn't do his work and who is not getting *A*s or *B*s or even *C*s; the student who is on the borderline or actually failing? Several action options are available. First, harass the student every day before the class for not doing his work. This technique in theory will shame him into doing it—if it doesn't exhaust the teacher first. (Of course, the teacher should not be surprised if the student develops a very special hatred for him.) Second, talk to the student and tell him that unless the homework is forthcoming consistently, his parents will be informed of his irresponsible performance. The easiest way out for the teacher is the third choice. Forget it! Give the student an *F* and write him off. Obviously, he doesn't want to learn anyway. But if the teacher is really concerned about his students, rather than merely with threatening or failing them, he would try to discover why the homework was not done. For example, some students have difficulty in reading that may have gone unnoticed; others have to work after school or in the evening to help support their family; some live in crowded conditions and thus are unable to study. Inquiry may reveal these and many other valid reasons for the student's apparent negligence.

Telling a student who is already failing a course that the missing homework will lower his grade is so absurd that one might wonder why it is ever done. Yet, there are far too many teachers who are so mesmerized by the power of the grade that they are unable to comprehend the child who does not fall down in fear at the thought of an *F* placed next to his name in that great book of books. Such a teacher appears to believe that the grade is the *end* in education.

Profanity

The teacher who welcomes student contributions in class discussions may suffer a severe shock when he discovers that the student's normal speech patterns includes profanity and obscenity commonly accepted by his peers and perhaps even permitted in his home. Women, particularly, sometimes find such language quite frightening. To most youngsters today, the use of certain four-letter words as a means of communication is completely natural and not meant to be offensive. It is part of their life style. They hear and use precisely the same descriptive language on the playground and in their own homes. Everyone understands what they have said. Yet, in school, they are told that such words are not acceptable. Who is wrong, the student or the teacher? In such situations, the usual implication is that one party *must* be wrong. Teachers who express this inflexible attitude will undoubtedly experience severe difficulty in dealing with certain types of students.

The authors remember two particular incidents which bear on this problem. Some years ago, in a program to sensitize teachers to the ways of different social classes of children, role-playing situations were utilized. One of the incidents called for the word *shit* to be used several times. The public school teachers in attendance were unable to cope realistically with this word in front of their peers (they could not even *say* the word!). Finally, two little nuns volunteered and played the roles perfectly. This word was prominent in the vocabulary of the students in their schools, and while they did not condone its usage, it did not render them helpless. More recently, while attending a conference on relevant teaching, a noted educator declared that the suppression of student's expression of four-letter words stifled his means of communication. He advocated that teachers be more interested in the ideas students have and less concerned with the vocabulary used in expressing them.

Such a liberal attitude could eventually do more harm than good. Our society appears ready to recognize a dichotomy of verbal communication between formal situations (school, job, and the like) and the informal situations (street, home, and so forth). A student who fails to realize which form of communication belongs with which form of activity or setting may be severely penalized in his relationships with others.

All this may be well and good, but how does it affect the

teacher? Most students know how they should speak in school. The teacher, upon hearing some particular word or phrase, who asks in a rather startled tone, "John, what did you say?" has probably made a serious mistake. John may, in all candor, repeat the remark, thus compounding the shock initially felt by the teacher (usually a woman) and alerting the entire class to the situation. A cautious teacher would not ask for a repeat performance. The word or phrase was heard clearly enough the first time. The question facing the teacher is simply what should be done.

It is important to know, of course, why or against whom the profanity was used. Teachers learn not to hear certain remarks that their students make. It is often a harmless way for students to let off steam, and the utterances are not directed to anyone. So perhaps after returning a set of test papers, it is best not to listen too intently as the students look at their grades since some who did not study may express their displeasure with themselves in their own unique way. The air may become a bit blue in some quarters. Most youngsters, especially by the time they reach high school, realize that certain words are not designed for classroom use. When they do utter some taboo word, more often than not it is simply a slip of the tongue and can safely be ignored by the teacher.

Profanity that is obviously and loudly directed at the teacher or at another student must be dealt with, and immediately. A teacher in this situation should not retaliate with similar language, nor should he show anger. This is often easier said than done. The student who is shouting abuse may be seeking attention from the teacher or approval from his peers. Or the youngster may have lost control of his own emotions; he may be expressing his anger and perhaps frustration by shouting and using shock words to express his rage.

If this is a situation of two students mutually abusing each other verbally, the teacher quickly interrupts the conversation, indicating plainly, firmly, and without anger that the show is over. It can be continued some other place and some other time. Then the teacher should proceed with the lesson without additional comment. There is no point in the teacher making any evaluation of the language that was used. It was really a private argument that simply happened to occur in the wrong place— the classroom.

If the youngster is striking at the teacher by using verbal abuse, the situation cannot be ignored. The first task is to prevent any more words from issuing forth beyond those already spoken.

Usually the student hollering some gem at the teacher will, once the word is out, stop dead in his tracks and wait for the reaction. The entire class will be waiting too.

Sometimes a firm, "That's enough, Susan," will suffice, and the lesson can continue without undue emphasis on the incident or unnecessary embarrassment to the student.

If the student is so angry (for whatever reason—and even the reason for such an action cannot be investigated at this point) that he continues to hurl abusive language in the teacher's general direction and ignores the command to cease and desist, then what? The student is too old for the teacher to hold his hand over the offender's mouth.

There may actually be no other alternative than permitting him to shout himself out. Eventually he will stop; although as the seconds drag by, the teacher may seriously doubt this. Finally when silence does return, there are several action options.

The student could be invited to visit the office of the assistant principal (for discipline) pronto and remain there until class is over and the teacher has the opportunity to discuss the matter. A note describing the incident should accompany the student. It is always best if the teacher can deal with the problem himself. Moving to a corner of the classroom and discussing the causes of the explosion might be best (by carefully arranging the teacher's desk, bookcases, and filing cabinet, some degree of privacy can be achieved for in-class conferences). There it can be determined whether or not the student should remain in class or go to some neutral corner in the school until he has cooled off. A visit to his guidance counselor could be the proper action option depending upon the student's state of mind. In any case, some action must be taken to stop the outburst, to deal with the offense and the offender, and to return the class to its prime purpose— learning.

For some reason unknown to Mr. Peterson, John suddenly began cursing and shouting abuse at him. From the startled look on the faces of the other students in the physical education class, they were as mystified by John's behavior as his teacher. Since he was unable to stop John's outburst, Mr. Peterson told the student to go to the principal's office and wait for him. When John, Mr. Peterson, and the principal met at the end of the period to discuss the incident, the student was apologetic and unable to explain his behavior. The principal decided that John should apologize to Mr. Peterson in front of the entire class. This idea was rejected by Mr. Peterson, who felt that the matter had been settled in their conference and a public apology would only serve to humiliate the student.

Behavior which is disruptive to the entire class cannot be permitted. Yet the behavior which the teacher rates as offensive and inappropriate (some teachers would be horrified if they heard a mild "damn") may seem to the student a normal and natural way of expressing anger and frustration. It is doubly important that the student understand and accept the reason why his offense is considered serious by the teacher. After taking action, the slate should be wiped clean. No mention need be made of the incident again. All too often, some teachers will goad a student by rather pointed reminders, which may just set him off anew. Once the issue has been resolved, forget about it.

Questions of Honesty

Although the use of profanity may disturb some teachers, breaches of trust between student and teacher will create a situation far more serious. Honesty is one area where most teachers are extremely sensitive and rigid. They expect their students to exhibit only the highest degree of integrity in all of their actions. Any deviation, no matter how slight, from this ideal may be considered not in the context of the actual situation but as a personal affront to the teacher and his standards. Cheating is cheating, lying is lying, and stealing is stealing—plain and simple. A student is either honest and truthful or dishonest and a liar. There can be no extenuating circumstances. Teacher flexibility in these areas is often nil. Violators are considered as rapidly headed for damnation (by way of the principal's office). Yet upon investigation, teachers may find that in matters of honesty, it is not always black or white; at times there are many gray areas. Therefore, although a student may cheat, lie, or steal, and thus offend the standards of middle-class morality, a careful examination could reveal circumstances which make crime more understandable.

S.I.R.S. (Student Information Retrieval System)   Test day could provide opportunities for problem situations to develop. The pop quiz (loved by teachers for its surprise effect and thus not to be condoned) places a student in a delicate position, should he happen to be unprepared on that particular day. He may be faced with two choices, cheating to survive—and possibly getting caught—or working on his own and receiving a poor grade which will lower his overall average. Neither option is very attractive.

Even the test announced weeks in advance, the one which will count 20 percent of the final grade, could also put a good student into such a panic that he feels a need to cheat. This student may really have studied hard for the test and entered the room feeling prepared. Then, upon reading the test questions he finds the teacher has selected areas which he considered unimportant and upon which he spent little study time.

Before exploring various techniques that could reduce cheating, it might be advantageous to examine the rationale behind this phenomenon in our schools. From first grade through graduate school, cheating is becoming a common occurrence. Why does anyone cheat? Pressure and panic seem to be the two most accepted reasons. Pressure exists to make the grade, which leads to the diploma, which opens the door to a good job, which provides a comfortable living. Panic that without the good grade, the important doors to a rewarding future will be closed—a rather appalling prospect at age eighteen or younger.

Add to this the fact that the youngster is not prepared for the test or sees the risk (the sheer excitement of trying to beat the teacher and get away with something) as more stimulating than studying. Nor should we overlook the hapless youngster who has not mastered the material and, like the drowning man, reaches for any straw.

The teacher should bear all of the guilt if he pops quizzes on his students or gives them no clues as to what is important in the 300 pages they have covered during the term. Some teachers delight in putting in obscure questions ("an A student should know everything") or in asking for so much information that no one could possibly complete the examination in the allotted time. Such teachers exert so much pressure that some adolescents react with behavior that teacher condemns as unacceptable. The student is then treated as a discipline problem.

The manner in which some examinations are given would also appear to be an open invitation to cheat. There are those teachers who feel that the honor system has almost vanished. Cynics point out "the teacher has the honor and the students have the system."

There are two major philosophies involved here concerning test administration. Some teachers feel that trust and respect on the part of the teacher will be repaid with honesty on the part of their students. They walk around the room after distributing the tests and are available to answer questions or explain obscure directions; even, on some occasions, to admit to an error on the test.

Such teachers are fully aware that not *all* students are worthy of trust and respect. One or two may take advantage of the situation to engage in a little information borrowing. However, the transgressions of a small minority of the class do not warrant treating the vast majority of students, who are quite honest, like common criminals. Since a test should not be considered or used as a tool for intimidation, these teachers feel no need to exert external controls over their students.

The other philosophy takes the opposite position. Teachers have an obligation to insure that honesty prevails during the taking of tests. They believe that the teacher who hands out tests and then retreats behind a book for the remainder of the period or who (nose down to the desk) grades papers seems an easy target to dupe. Since it appears that the teacher's eyes are confined to one given area, the eyes of some students may soon begin a wide sweep of the general vicinity for some answer assistance.

Certain types of questions asked on tests facilitate this action. Teachers who rely solely on multiple-choice statements or true-false questions are remembered daily in the prayers of those students who espouse the new morality of "everybody cheats—why be different."

Some students have developed the concept of instant information retrieval to a veritable art. Answers may be concealed on a facial tissue. Then, one sneeze and it's "goodby, evidence" should the teacher suddenly make a circuit of the room. Others prefer the answer written on an eraser. Removing the evidence is accomplished with a quick rub.

Many students resent cheating by their classmates and feel the teacher is not meeting his responsibilities when he permits it to occur. There is justification for this feeling. If the test is important (of course, all tests are important—otherwise why bother?), it should be undertaken in an atmosphere which permits every student an equal opportunity for success. This is not the case if one youngster is able to use his notes or text for assistance. If a teacher has reason to believe this might happen, he should position himself in the back of the room once the test has been distributed. Here he can observe the proceedings unobtrusively. The students will be well aware of his presence and any movement on their part will be quickly noted by the teacher.

In spite of all precautions, a student may still be caught cheating. Several action options are available to the teacher when this happens. Some teachers refuse to see a student cheating, thus avoiding an unpleasant confrontation. Besides, what can he really do? He can loudly accuse the student—"John, are you cheating?" John will deny all, and in the meantime every other student's chain of thought has been broken. If the teacher does not believe John (it is the teacher's word against his), he could tear up John's paper triumphantly for the class to witness. Or perhaps the student could be told to stop writing because his paper will not be accepted; furthermore, he should remain after class to discuss the matter. (Both these techniques will be highly embarrassing to the student and thus cannot be recommended.) A variation of this plan is to say nothing during class but have him report after class for a discussion of the teacher's observation.

All these procedures raise interesting questions. Is the student receiving due process? Can a teacher call a student a cheat, tear up his paper, and record a failure in the grade book? Must the teacher have any tangible proof?

The best approach to the problem is to develop a classroom atmosphere which makes cheating unnecessary. A student should feel free to talk with his teacher whenever he is having difficulty in his studies. Although this might be considered heresy, a teacher might actually permit a student to take a test at a later date if the student were making academic progress but was not ready for the exam at that time. Why force a student who is trying to succeed to take a test at a time when he has little chance for success?

Then, should cheating occur despite the teacher's attempts to work with his students, some decisive action is warranted. A zero on the test plus a warning might suffice. A discussion with the guidance counselor could give the teacher valuable clues as to the reason behind this behavior. Perhaps the student has developed a pattern indicating a possible psychological disorder. Or the cheating may be confined to that particular teacher's class and, therefore, is a breakdown in the teacher-student relationship in which the student feels unable to talk with his teacher. Should this appear to be the case, the teacher should reexamine his behavior in dealing with the student.

Untruths (What's really true?)   Another possible source of friction between teacher and student which could lead to discipline problems is the lie. Most teachers believe they are receptive and that their students should feel free to tell them the truth. Should they discover that a student has lied to them, it is a shock to their self-image. This is examining the problem from a purely personal point of view. What the teacher should ask is why the student felt the necessity to lie to him.

> Peggy had missed home economics class on Wednesday, but her name had not appeared on the absentee list. When she returned on Thursday, Mrs. Graham asked her where she had been. Peggy explained that she had stayed to talk with her shorthand teacher about a personal matter and would bring a note the following day.
>
> After several days and still no note, Peggy finally told Mrs. Graham that she had talked with her shorthand teacher, but only for a few minutes. Then, feeling ill, she went to the nurse's office but no one was there. She spent the remainder of the period in the Girls' Room.
>
> Although Peggy had violated a school rule by not going to the main office when the health suite was closed, Mrs. Graham was more concerned that Peggy had been unable to tell her the truth.

To some students, truth is what appears beneficial to their cause without amplification on the more personally detrimental aspects. "What he doesn't know, won't hurt *me*" seems to be the motto of those who are unable to confide in their teacher because they are uncertain of how he will react to the truth.

The adolescent who appears to be developing a pattern of lying should be of grave concern to the teacher and to all adults who work with him. In extreme cases, such behavior may be an outward symptom of a possible emotional disorder if reality is so painful that it must be remade constantly.

Others will lie in their need to gain recognition or approval— even if approval is of only a temporary nature. Often when confronted with the falsity of their statements, they may shrug and say, "Well, it was worth a try." Dealing with such youngsters is extremely difficult. Teachers should exercise great care and discretion before accusing a student of lying. Even with an air-tight case, it is not necessary to conduct a 20th-century version of the Inquisition (with the class watching), nor will it get to the cause of the behavior. Should the teacher later be proved wrong, the student is certainly entitled to a formal apology. After all, the student undoubtedly denied the charges and his teacher still failed to believe him. Whatever rapport had previously been established between them will be greatly damaged if not destroyed by the episode.

In dealing with matters of truth, it is always important for the teacher to consider the possible causes of the student's actions. The teacher's goal should be the discovery and alleviation of the pressures that forced the adolescent to consider truth an undesirable response. To accomplish this the teacher will need to know why the student was unable to trust him. Perhaps it was his attitude that made the student believe he was uninterested in him as an individual. Before the teacher is able to help the student, he may have to reexamine their previous relationship.

Permanent Borrowing (Whatsa matter? Ya lose somethin'?) Every teacher quickly learns that almost any object, regardless of its size, if left unattended can vanish within seconds without leaving a trace. Part of this phenomenon stems from the type of articles brought to school. The second phase of this problem is the careless manner in which some students care for their valuables. Items are forgotten and left on the lunch table or desk. Usually by the time the student remembers that he has left his radio under his desk in Mr. Johnson's class it has disappeared. Alas, the temptation is just too great for some students to resist. In this sense, petty theft is facilitated by carelessness.

The teacher himself often becomes the target for those suffering from sticky fingers. Usually, the loss is money—often funds collected for the school newspaper, a charity drive, field trip, or other worthy cause. Naturally (despite repeated warnings from the administration about leaving money in the classroom) the teacher had the funds in the unlocked top drawer of his desk. What is he to do? This is money entrusted to him by the students for some specific purpose. Most teachers find that their penance for such deviations from the world of reality is to replace the missing money with their own hard-earned cash. Rarely has a teacher had money stolen from his desk twice.

Besides money, teachers also find that school equipment, charged to them, is apt to disappear. Chemistry teachers often discover that their lab materials seem to vanish into thin air. Paperback books are another easy target if the teacher is not careful. One school, having a shortage of textbooks, would not permit the books to leave the building. To their dismay, a book blackmarket emerged within the school. Texts were smuggled from the storage room and sold to students. Since no one officially was supposed to have a textbook in his possession, those who purchased books had to keep them at home. Yet they felt by having a text of their own they had an academic advantage over their classmates who were without one.

> When questioned by the principal as to why he ordered more paperback books each year than any other teacher on the staff, Mr. Bellows, a 10th-grade basic English teacher stated that the books were taken by the students. The suggestions to keep a closer check on the books was vetoed by Mr. Bellows. He felt that when low-ability students were sufficiently interested in books to permanently "borrow" them, his English program was successful.

Catching the thief or retrieving the lost merchandise is at best a lost cause. Thefts of equipment are reported to the office (a matter of school policy) and duly recorded. But this does not bring about a return of the item or apprehend the crook. Teachers often announce that a particular object is missing and call for its return. Now, no child in his right mind is going to stand up and admit, "I stole that, Mrs. Wright." So, teachers have devised various means for allowing the missing item to reappear with no questions asked. This is the best approach if the return of the goods is the primary objective. It is a slick trick if the teacher can catch the thief and retrieve the goods all in one fell swoop. However, the chances of success are extremely remote.

In the case of missing money that has been in the teacher's care, several motives should be considered. Did the student need the money for a date, gassing up his car, food (many students never receive enough to eat), or clothes so that he would have something to wear to school or to be as well dressed as his classmates? Did he take it on a dare? Was the theft an act of hostility against the teacher (to make him look bad in front of the class) and the amount of money taken of no real consequence to the thief? The teacher should consider these factors before determining which is more important, the return of the money or the capture of the student thief.

Lecturing about honesty being the best policy is a waste of time. Some youths have spent their entire lives appropriating what they need to make their existence more bearable. In some cases, they are even encouraged by their parents (either openly or by their looking the other way) to take what they want since there is little hope that family finances will ever be sufficient to care for them adequately. This is a tragic reality of our society.

Television with its distortions of life further accentuates the differences between the haves and the have nots, leaving a segment of our society embittered and frustrated.

Caution will be the only protection against stealing. Students should be warned not to bring valuables to school, not to leave their lockers unlocked, nor to share their locker combinations with others. Girls should be reminded to keep their purses with them at all times and in a position where items cannot be removed without being seen. Finally, the teacher should set the example and not tempt weak-willed students by permitting money or school property to be taken easily.

Vandalism

Of mounting concern in the schools is vandalism. Part of the problem stems from some students' lack of identification with the school. Adolescents who like their school and who feel the school wants them to be there will not vandalize it. Helping to instill a feeling of pride (this is *my* school; here I am welcome and important) is part of a teacher's job.

Just why students choose to deface property has been the concern of many psychologists examining adolescent behavior though no remedies have been developed to curb all such activities. It may be done out of boredom (the curriculum is uninteresting to many students), thoughtlessness (many youths do not take care of their own property), or perhaps for kicks by the frustrated or angry student who can see no future for himself or chance for success in school.

Occasionally, vandalism is committed against the property of another student. If this happens during the class ("Bill just drew a dirty picture on my notebook cover!" or "Mary broke my watch!"), learning may cease until the issue has been settled. Rather than devote class time to the problem, the matter can be handled after the period or at the close of school. At that time the teacher can weigh the factors involved in the case and render his decision.

Undoubtedly, to the teacher the worst form of vandalism is the malicious damaging of his own personal property. Teachers' cars have been scratched, convertible tops cut, tires slashed, and radio antennas bent or broken by disgruntled students. Naturally a car parked in the faculty parking lot is the easiest personal item to damage if a student feels that he has to get even with a teacher. In some cases, students have even visited a teacher's home and broken windows, littered the lawn, thrown paint on the house, turned over trash cans, or damaged shrubbery.

It is difficult to excuse this under the heading of youthful high jinks. It is also extremely difficult to discover and prove who is responsible. Sometimes even the true motive is obscured. When personal property is involved, the principal should be informed and the police notified. Beyond that, there is very little that the teacher can do.

Violence

One of the more frightening aspects of teaching today is the rising number of physical assaults on teachers by students. With newspapers capitalizing on each violent incident in the schools, many a teacher (both beginning and experienced) wonders whether it is really worth it to be a teacher. Even though the chances of physical attack by a secondary school student upon any individual teacher are still relatively small, they are occurring with alarming frequency.

In a discussion of this problem with a graduate class composed of teachers, one of the authors was informed by three of the students that assaults had taken place in each of their schools within a week's time. In one case a woman teacher had her arm severely twisted behind her back by a student. A male teacher was hit on the head with a chair. Another male teacher was punched in the face. In all incidents the students involved were punished. Each received a *three-day suspension* from school. Penalties this light are nothing more than a token and will not deter violence against teachers.

Today the problem of violence in the schools has become even more complex. For one thing, students realize that teachers are afraid of being sued. Everyone knows that a teacher is never expected to strike a minor, even in self-defense. This is not a new attitude. Teachers have always run a considerable legal risk even when defending themselves. However, the problem is highlighted now by the students' awareness that school administrators are hesitant to invoke the once-used ultimate weapon of expulsion. Now the punishment is more of a slap-on-the-wrist type, which is proving to be a very poor deterrent to violence. So, while this is a student-caused problem, it is often encouraged by a lack of firm administrative retaliation.

This knowledge will be of little consolation to a teacher who suddenly finds himself under physical attack. What should he do?

Common sense would dictate that the teacher protect himself. Yet how far does one go in doing this? The answer should be: Just far enough to protect himself from harm while using as little force as possible (realizing all the time the legal implications of touching a student). The threat to the teacher's health should determine his actions. The petite girl who slaps or attempts to slap the burly male teacher can be ignored as a physical threat to his well-being. The teacher does not need to exert any force to protect himself. He should be able to contain the student without harming her and permit the administrative procedures of the school to deal with her actions.

In many cases, violence which occurs is brought into the school by a nonstudent. This is a problem that is becoming increasingly difficult to solve. One teacher was struck in the face when he attempted to stop a fight between a student and youth who had entered the school grounds. A twenty-five-year-old woman teacher was raped in a school storage room by a youth who had entered the building and was hiding there. The invasion of school property by youths who do not belong there is a problem which must be faced by both teachers and administrators. Each has a responsibility to insure that only persons on school business are permitted on the grounds and in the building.

At times teachers stumble into violent situations. Occasionally, they will be called upon to break up a fight between two boys or even between girls. Student fighting can frequently be stopped by a firm and loud verbal command. If the teacher attempts to separate the combatants, he runs the risk of being struck by a stray blow. As a result, many teachers will not enter the fray without assistance from another teacher or member of the administration staff. Again, care should be taken to protect the youthful sluggers from accidental injury during the separation process.

Threats of physical violence can also be frightening to teachers, especially to women. Such occurrences are relatively rare; but if the teacher feels that the threat is genuine and not the grumbling of a disgruntled student, the matter should be brought to the attention of the administration immediately. For the male teacher to accept a challenge hurled by a student ("One of these days you and I are going to meet away from the school . . .") is not only stupid but financially risky. The teacher really has nothing to gain and everything to lose. He is not paid to go ten rounds with his students or to prove that he is the toughest guy in class. It would be far better to advise the student's parents about his threats. Of course, the student should be apprised of the consequences of making threats and, even worse, of carrying them out; this will hopefully deter him from acting.

Drugs

The newest and in many respects the most awesome problem facing the teacher today is that of drugs. "The use of drugs, particularly marijuana, is now an accepted fact of life for anywhere from 30 to 50 percent of all U.S. secondary school students."[6] Some students who smoke pot prior to or during the school day claim that it reduces their feeling of pressure. Others begin their experience with drugs to win peer approval.

Irrespective of the reason, these students are in school. "The use of drugs is so common that students are contemptuous of those who overindulge. The pothead who gets stoned quietly is accepted as a normal part of the school scene, but the showoffs are put down."[7]

The question facing the teacher is twofold. If the student is not disruptive in class, does the teacher have a legal or moral obligation to report a suspected drug user? If so, to whom should the student be reported? The administration? The student's parents? The school nurse? The police? If the student is a user of drugs and some official notification is made by his teacher, a possible criminal record could be the result. With this in mind, many teachers are hesitant to take any action beyond advising the school nurse who works with student drug users in some schools.

> The Problems of Democracy class was discussing the limitations of the monarchy as a form of government. Mr. Edgar, a new teacher and the second member of a three-teacher 12th-grade social studies team, noticed that Steve, who was participating in the discussion at every opportunity, was becoming so relaxed he appeared almost unable to remain upright in his chair. Yet Steve's contributions were logical and useful.
>
> During the showing of a film in the latter part of the period, Mr. Edgar asked Mr. Parkhurst, the senior member of the team, about Steve. "Oh, can't you tell? He's stoned again. I don't know why Mrs. Anderson (the third member of the teaching team, who was conducting the discussion that day) keeps calling on him when he's that way."

[6]"The Drug Scene: High Schools are Higher Now," *Newsweek* 75, No. 7 (February 16, 1970): 66. Copyright Newsweek, Inc., February 16, 1970.
[7]*Ibid.*, 67.

Since the heavy use of drugs is a relatively recent problem in our secondary schools, teachers appear to be uncertain how to cope with the problem. If the student is not disturbing anyone, the tendency may be to ignore the situation rather than venture into the unknown. This attitude may change as new teachers enter the profession either having known drug users among their peers or having experimented with drugs themselves during their college days.

At present, guidelines for disseminating complete and accurate information concerning drugs and the legal consequences of using drugs are being handled by school guidance departments.[8] How successful this type of approach will be remains to be seen.

If some students are using drugs to reduce the pressures of school, then it would appear that teachers have a primary responsibility to emphasize student self-growth and deemphasize the pressure of grades as a measure of success.

Summary

Our focus in this chapter has been on the student. We investigated the pressures and problems that face the adolescent in his search for identity in our rapidly changing society.

Then we turned our attention to those irritations that can effectively frustrate the teacher and disrupt a class and how to handle these minor irritations before they become major ones.

The reasons why students fail to fulfill their responsibilities were examined. Teacher reactions to student profanity, stealing, and vandalism were also analyzed. We explored the various action options which a teacher could utilize to protect himself or students against personal injury. Finally the drug menace and its implications for the teacher were presented.

Thus we have tried to spotlight the problems that the student may bring into the classroom to impede—or even halt—the teaching-learning process.

Situations Caused by Students

The following pages present actual discipline situations that were caused by some action taken by the student.

[8]Robert F. Aubrey, "Student Drug Use and the Responsibility of Guidance Personnel," *Focus on Guidance* 2 (October, 1969): 2.

Situation 1: "Shame on You!"   All the students were at their lab stations working on an experiment. Mr. Still, the teacher, was going from student to student checking their progress and offering assistance if needed. He had just finished talking with Ginger Williams and was turning to go when suddenly Ginger jumped, grabbed her bottom, and exclaimed, "Mr. Still! Shame on you!"

The class looked up from their work and laughed. Ginger smiled, rubbed the injured area, and returned to her microscope. Mr. Still looked dumbfounded. He had not touched her. What did the class think? What was she trying to do? Turning to the class he . . .

Action Options

1. . . . decided to ignore the situation and go to the next student.

2. . . . explained that he had never touched Ginger.

3. . . . asked Ginger to explain exactly what she meant by her comments and actions.

Situation 2: "Where, Oh, Where Did My Little Student Go?"   On the day of the semester exam Janice was among the missing but her name was not listed on the official absentee sheet. The following day she told Mr. Phillips, her math teacher, that she had a very serious personal problem (which she was not at liberty to reveal at that time) and had spent the entire class period with her guidance counselor.

That afternoon in the teacher's lounge, Mr. Phillips mentioned Janice's absence to the counselor, adding that he hoped the problem had been solved.

"What problem?" asked the counselor. "Janice just dropped in for about 30 seconds to change her schedule for next year."

Mr. Phillips explained the story to the counselor, adding that now he was going to . . .

Action Options
   1. . . . confront Janice with the lie and request a full explanation.

   2. . . . tell Janice that for missing the test without a valid excuse she will receive an F.

Situation 3: "Did You Lose It?"   Art appeared to be a most conscientious student when he first reported to Mr. Patterson's class at the beginning of the term. Even before the first assignment was made, he had inquired about doing extra credit work. As the term progressed, the work he submitted was satisfactory but was always late.

The first time, he told Mr. Patterson that he had done his assignment but left it on the hall table at home and would bring it in tomorrow. Tomorrow proved to be two weeks and two reminders later.

Art was consistently tardy with his homework, but he always had a plausible excuse. On one occasion, he even presented a note from his mother stating he was unable to do the assignment because the entire family attended a funeral.

When the big term paper was due, Art's was missing. When asked why, Art insisted that he had turned the paper in. "I put it right on your desk as I went out, don't you remember? Maybe you lost it."

"Now wait a minute, Art," Mr. Patterson told him, "I have 150 students and 149 term papers got into my hands safely. Doesn't it seem strange to you that your paper would be the only one lost?"

"Gee, I wouldn't know about that," replied Art, "all I know is that I turned it in and it was a good paper. I'm sure it was worth at least a *B*. What are you going to do about my grade, Mr. Patterson?" Faced with this situation, Mr. Patterson should . . .

Action Options
    1. . . . accept Art's word and gave him a *B* on the paper.

    2. . . . accuse Art of lying, of not handing in the paper, and give him a zero.

3. . . . tell Art he will recheck and see if the paper has been misplaced.

4. . . . tell Art he must do the paper again if it is not found.

5. . . . accept Art's word, but give no grade (nor exact any penalty) for the missing paper.

6. . . . (your solution)

Situation 4: "What Did You Say?"   Jane Winston waited while her class entered the room. It was the first day of school and she was watching each student carefully as they came in and selected a desk. The last to enter was a large, sloppy boy who went to the far corner of the room. Sliding down in the seat, he stretched his long legs out into the aisle. He appeared to be more reclining than sitting.

When the bell rang for the class to begin, all students were looking to the front waiting for her first words—all except the large boy in the back. His eyes were closed.

"You, in the back, sit up and pay attention," she commanded.

"Go screw yourself," came the response.

"What did you say?"

"I said, 'Go screw yourself.' "

The class looked first at the boy and then at Miss Winston. She could feel the students waiting for her to respond. It was her move. What a way to start the school year! At this point, the only thing she could do was . . .

Action Options
1. . . . pretend that she did not understand what the student said and ignore the statement.

2. . . . demand an instant apology.

3. ... send the boy to the office with a note explaining the situation.

4. ... go to the office herself and request something be done about this student.

5. ... blush and tell the boy that gentlemen do not talk that way to ladies.

6. ... (your solution)

Situation 5: "Teacher Beware!"   Miss Wilson, a first-year teacher, had experienced considerable difficulty in controlling several boys in her American history class who delighted in making smart remarks during the lessons. Finally John, the leader of the group, seemed to change. He began to drop by the classroom after school; he turned in his homework on time, and, in general, he settled down during the class period. His buddies followed this example. When John was good and cooperative, so were they.

Being intelligent, John had little trouble in doing *A* work once he decided to stop deviling Miss Wilson. His friends were not as academically inclined but were able to earn average grades.

Miss Wilson was pleased with the change. She had always liked John. He was difficult not to like even at his tormenting best. At the end of the first grading period, she asked him to stop by her room after school. She informed him that she was pleased with his attitude and work and that he had earned an *A* for the term. John did not appear to share her enthusiasm about his progress.

"How did my buddies do?" he inquired.

"You know that I can't discuss their grades, John."

"Okay," John replied, "Just so they get *A*s too."

"But what if they didn't do *A* work?"

"Who cares! If you want me to remain your friend, my friends had better get *A*s."

Confused by John's attitude, Miss Wilson . . .

Action Options

1. . . . tells John that his friends will get *A*s also.

2. . . . explains that grades are earned, not given.

3. ... tells John off in no uncertain terms and leaves him with the decision concerning his own behavior.

4. ... asks him not to spoil his good record by doing something foolish.

5. ... (your solution)

Situation 6: "Nobody Better Try To Stop Me!"   Tom, a junior, seemed to fit the perfect movie stereotype of a hood. He was 6-feet 4 inches tall with long, black, greasy hair and a sullen expression. He had been in trouble with the police and was currently on probation for his latest escapade, stealing a car. Among the students he had a poor reputation and most of his teachers considered him a troublemaker. On one occasion, he had been suspended for striking a teacher.

In Mr. Zelinski's class, however, Tom had never caused any trouble. He just sat quietly and stared out of the window. One day just as the class was finishing their discussion, the bell rang. Mr. Zelinski asked the class to remain seated for a minute so that he could complete his comments.

Suddenly Tom, whose desk was on the aisle nearest to the door jumped up, "I'm leaving *now* and nobody better try to stop me."

Surprised by Tom's action, Mr. Zelinski . . .

Action Options

1. . . . stood in the doorway and dared Tom to knock him over.

2. . . . ordered Tom to be seated until he finished and dismissed the class.

3. ... stepped out of Tom's way without saying a word.

4. ... sent Tom to the principal's office for being rude and insolent.

5. ... sent a note to the principal's office informing him of Tom's action.

6. ... (your solution)

Suggested Readings

Blackham, Garth J. *The Deviant Child in the Classroom.* Belmont, Calif.: Wadsworth Publishing Co. Inc., 1967. Although the book is oriented toward the younger child, the material also applies to the secondary student.

Dodson, Dan W. *High School Racial Confrontation: A Study of the White Plains, New York, Student Boycott.* New York: The White Plains Board of Education, 1969. Description of the events which led to the boycott and how the incidents were handled by the administration with implications for improving faculty-student-administration relations.

Leonard, George B. "Testing Vs. Your Child." *Look* 30, No. 6 (March 22, 1966): 63–64, 66, 67. Why students cheat and instructional techniques which foster or reduce cheating.

MacLennan, Beryce W. "Scapegoating." *Today's Education* 58, No. 6 (September, 1969): 38–40. Discusses scapegoating as a response to frustration in the classroom.

Madsen, Charles H., Jr., and Madsen, Clifford. *Teaching/Discipline: Behavioral Principles Toward a Positive Approach.* Boston: Allyn & Bacon, Inc., 1970. A behavior modification approach to various student problems at all school levels.

Morse, William C. "Disturbed Youngsters in the Classroom." *Today's Education* 58, No. 4 (April, 1969): 30–37. Explores the serious problems of emotionally disturbed children in the classroom with suggestions for dealing with them.

National Education Association. *Discipline in the Classroom.* Washington, D.C.: National Education Association, 1969. Selected cases of misbehavior in the classroom, illustrated examples of good disciplinary techniques, and discussion of effective classroom control.

Peters, R. S. *Ethics and Education.* Glenview, Ill.: Scott, Foresman, and Company, 1966. Chap. 9. Examines types of punishment and limitations of each in terms of deterrent and prevention and reformative effect on the individual.

Public Information Branch and Center for Studies of Narcotics and Drug Abuse. "Students and Drug Abuse." *To-*

day's Education 58, No. 3 (March, 1969) : 35–50. Discusses best-known drugs and narcotics used by adolescents.

Redl, Fritz. "Aggression in the Classroom." *Today's Education* 58, No. 1 (September, 1969) : 30–31. Discusses causes of aggression and appropriate teacher responses.

Wesley, Donald A. "Prevent Cheating." *The Clearing House* 39, No. 4 (December, 1964) : 233–234. Some useful suggestions to help teachers physically limit classroom cheating.

4

Administrator-Caused Problems

This chapter will focus on the secondary school administrator and the various ways he may act as a catalyst between teachers and students resulting in discipline problems.

The administration, depending upon the size of the school, may consist of a principal and from one to four assistant principals. As the school board's agent, the principal is legally responsible for operating the school with a maximum of efficiency and a minimum of expense and trouble. The principal is also expected to provide quality education for students of diverse social, economic, racial, and religious backgrounds. He is faced with students who do not want to be in school at all and those who aspire to attend Ivy League colleges. It is his job to attempt to satisfy each unique educational need. Added to these problems, the principal often finds that his school must be severely overcrowded (because of lack of funds to build additional classrooms). These conditions may necessitate restricting student movement, limiting co-curricular activities, and taxing the proximity tolerance of both students and teachers. So if it appears that he sometimes exerts considerable pressure on his staff and students, it may be that he is struggling to combat the growing list of pressures and demands placed on him. Parents, students, members of the school board, the superintendent, and various community groups may be only a few of the voices bringing causes, complaints, and charges before him which must be settled immediately and with complete satisfaction. The rather simplistic view of the principal as the iron-fisted, stern-visaged authority who punished the bad and graduated the good is now changed.[1]

However, it cannot be denied that the personal philosophy of the administrator concerning discipline will affect both teachers and students, for it is within this framework that they are all expected to function. Here is where problems often develop.

A principal who takes a paternalistic or authoritarian view of the administration of his school is likely to superimpose rules which students and teachers are expected to follow. Students object to regulations that appear to them archaic, irrelevant, and restrictive. Many feel that they should be consulted and have an active voice in determining the policies that directly affect them.

Often teachers have ambivalent feelings about administrative regulations. Some seek a more active part in the formulation of disciplinary procedures, feeling that arbitrary decisions that overlook faculty and student opinion create classroom problems. Others prefer to hide behind the protective screen of administrative sanctions rather than to become involved with students and their values. Perhaps each teacher should ask himself the purpose of the various rules within his school and if they will most effectively contribute to the total growth of the adolescent. If, in the teacher's opinion, a rule serves no useful purpose, does he have any responsibility to himself and to his students to become involved and serve as an agent for change? Each teacher must answer this question for himself.

Running the Bureaucratic Maze

Many principals run a tight ship, believing that a school engulfed in red tape is safe, secure, and happy because everyone knows where he is, or where he is going since there is a form or rule to guide him. So a trap has been set which may eventually snare

---

[1] For a principal's point of view on what's wrong with schools and how they should be operated, see Leslie A. Hart, *The Classroom Disaster*, New York: Teachers College Press, 1969.

student and teacher alike. Any teacher new to the school will spend the first three or four days just learning to identify the mountain of forms and learning the rules required to move students within the school, like so many pieces on a chessboard. Usually, it will require months of practice and frequent referral to the *Teacher's Handbook* to learn when and why to use each form.

Take the case of absences, for example. In many schools, a returning student is expected to present a note from his parents (written in ink, never in pencil) explaining why he was absent. Incidentally, try to explain *that* school policy to an irate parent who pencilled a note while hurrying to work, was late himself, and then was told by his offspring that evening the note was no good. But assuming that the note was properly prepared, the teacher must scrutinize its contents and decide whether the absence was valid. (Parents also resent this: "Who is your teacher to say that the excuse *I* wrote is not valid!") Should the student have forgotten his excuse or should the teacher deem the excuse unacceptable, the student is given an Unexcused Absence slip (green) which must be replaced by the coveted Excused Absence slip (blue) by the next day or he will not be permitted to enter class.

Many students quietly resent these procedures, which seem to them an indication of lack of trust by the faculty. Others react so negatively to a procedure which appears to waste their time and run them around in circles that their frustration at the "system" may boil over in anger against the unsuspecting classroom teacher who enforces this regulation. At best, students question how some regulations actually relate to learning, which is their purpose for being in school. A good example of this was reported in *Saturday Review*.

> . . . The other day this other guy and I had to make up an English test we'd missed because we were absent. The English teacher said she'd give it to us at 8 o'clock in the morning before school begins. Well, I knew that if the test made me late for my homeroom period at 8:30, that teacher would send down an absent slip on me to the office. So I went to my homeroom at five of 8 and wrote a note on the blackboard to the teacher, telling her where I was and that I might be late.
>
> This other guy, though, he didn't know enough to do that. He hasn't studied the system. So we go and make up our test and sure enough before we are through the late bell rings for homeroom period. I can see he's nervous and he doesn't know what to do, so he tries to hurry up and

finish the test so he can get to his homeroom before the absent slips get sent down. He tears through the test and probably marks half the multiple-choices wrong. Then he takes off just as the first bell for first period is ringing.

I saw him later in the day and he was all shook up. He couldn't catch the absent slips so he had to go down to the office of the dean of boys to explain that he wasn't really tardy or absent. But the dean's office had a long line, and while the guy's waiting in line, the late bell for the first period rings. So now he's half-way out of his mind, you know? By the time he gets up to the dean of boys, he really *is* late for first period and another absent slip about him is already on its way down from *that* teacher. The dean of boys tells him to come in for detention after school, one hour.

. . . Well, the guy gets all uptight and tries to explain why he now has two absent slips going when he wasn't even tardy. He loses his cool and says some things and the dean says some things and the next thing you know, the guy's got *two* hours detention, for being rude and smart-alecky. But wait, it gets worse. I swear he hasn't got a brain, that kid. Anyway, as it happens, the day he was absent and missed the English test, he also missed a math test. And he's scheduled to make that one up after school, when he's supposed to be in the detention hall. If he misses the math test, it won't be given again, and he doesn't know if his grade can stand a zero for this mark-ing period. But if he misses detention, he might be sus-pended and have three days' worth of stuff to make up when he gets back.

I don't know what he did, finally. Probably just had a nervous breakdown. It was really pathetic. But the point is that he should have foreseen all that and made arrange-ments for it. I'll be surprised if he makes it through school. He just doesn't understand the system.[2]

Still, the large number of students in secondary schools and the legal necessity to account for these students force schools to maintain some system for keeping a record of those present. States reimburse school districts on the basis of how many stu-dents appear in school each day. As a result, body-counting is, in effect, a money-making concern for the school. Many teachers and students do not understand this. If principals would take

[2]Kathryn Johnston Noyes and Gordon L. McAndrew, "Is This What Schools Are For?" *Saturday Review* (December 21, 1968), p. 59. Copyright 1968 Saturday Review, Inc.

time to explain the reasons behind a regulation, compliance might be achieved with considerably less tension on the part of those affected by the rule.

Another regulation that many teachers and students question is the use of a hall pass. In some schools *any* movement within the building must follow a carefully prescribed pattern. No student can venture forth into the hallway without an identifying pass issued by his teacher certifying that he has a valid reason to be in the halls at that minute. Following the regulation to the letter, some teachers believe it is their duty to question rigorously the reasons given by students for wanting to leave the classroom. Fortunately, other teachers attempt to place the regulation in the proper perspective. Rather than question and possibly embarrass a student, they make the hall pass available to use as needed. This says to the student that he is trusted and that his teacher believes that this privilege will not be abused.

Just as a teacher's individual classroom regulations should be examined periodically to see that they are still valid, so should schoolwide rules be reviewed regularly by a joint committee of faculty, students, and administrators. Perhaps the question should be "Is this regulation the best way to achieve the desired results with a minimum of inconvenience and irritation to those concerned?"

The Enforcers

Many teachers feel they should not be compelled to act as policemen or enforcers while administrators, charged with the safety and maintenance of the school, feel faculty should share in this responsibility. For example, administrators, in their efforts to adhere to school board policy, ask teachers not to pass a restroom without going in to check for student smokers. How should a teacher react to a rule such as this? Unfortunately some teachers seem to delight in catching students, feeling that they gain in stature through this exercise of power. Others may question the regulation reasoning that a student caught in this way is likely to feel the teacher's only purpose in entering the restroom was to apprehend someone breaking the school rule and make trouble for him. The rapport between such a student and his teacher may be severely affected. Furthermore, the student may seek some means of retaliating through deviant behavior in the classroom. What is a student to think when everywhere he turns it appears that a teacher is watching and waiting for him to break a rule?

> Mr. Partridge was going down the hall when he saw Alice standing by the water fountain. She had just unwrapped what appeared to be a mint. "I'll take that, young lady. You know eating is not permitted in the halls.
>
> Alice tried to protest saying that it was medicine for her ulcer. Mr. Partridge took the "mint." "Seventh graders do not have ulcers," he told her.

Even in the parking lot, it is believed a student will get himself into trouble. Teachers are assigned to make certain that no one goes near a car (especially those belonging to the faculty) during the lunch periods. Even student cars need watching. Some students have been known to go to their cars for a quick smoke. Boys and girls at times will even forsake lunch for a little good lovin' in a parked car. So the principal delegates the responsibility to the faculty for making certain that no funny business occurs in his parking lot. Such an arrangement adversely affects the morale of students and teachers, further straining the rapport between them as each receives an unfavorable image of the other.

Dress Codes ("What do you mean a cocktail dress is inappropriate in school?")   Those schools having dress codes may place teachers in the unenviable position of serving as an arbiter of taste. They are told to check the length of skirts; make certain boys have their shirt tails tucked in; determine whether a young lady's sweater or dress is too tight or provocative or revealing, or if a boy's jeans are too tight or his hair is too long. Teachers who criticize a student's clothes even in private may find the parent descending upon them demanding to know by what right the teacher presumed to dictate how his child should be dressed. Besides, what male teacher is going to admit that he was looking at a young girl's legs (how else can he determine if the skirt is too short), or that after careful examination has decided that her blouse is cut too low, or that he finds her provocative. Any male teacher who backs himself into that type of corner will find his girl-watchers membership revoked (maybe even his teaching certificate also).

Should the teacher be so foolish as to attack a particular student's style of dress before the entire class, he can expect any rapport previously enjoyed with that student to be severely damaged, if not completely destroyed. Furthermore, the other students in the class will react negatively to the teacher's remarks.

Hence, he will have created a hostile classroom atmosphere, a breeding ground for possible discipline problems.

If, in the teacher's opinion, the student has broken the dress code, then perhaps a private discussion is in order. It might even be better from the standpoint of rapport between student and teacher to refer the matter to the counselor (avoiding the principal if possible so that it does not become a disciplinary matter). Using class time for a discussion of a student's attire only alienates the persons with whom the teacher must work and wastes everyone's time. Besides, is this the teacher's job? Though some research[3] supports the position that the way a student dresses influences his behavior in class, many teachers refuse to become involved as critics in matters of dress, reasoning that it can only harm their rapport with students and that they are not in a position to judge what is proper or improper except as it interferes with the teaching-learning process.

When we think of teachers objecting to student attire, the usual picture that comes to mind is the adolescent who is dirty or wearing way-out clothing. Just the opposite occurred recently. A young woman teacher complained that the girls in her 10th-grade class were *too well dressed*. They made *her* feel sloppy and uncomfortable.

Any teacher who finds himself unduly disturbed by the way students dress should perhaps question why he considers appearance of such critical importance. Many students feel that their mode of dress is a means of expressing their individuality. If a teacher is criticizing a student's clothing, he is, in the student's mind, criticizing him as an individual.

While some schools have simply stated "Wear what you like," assuming that parents approve what is worn, others have solved this problem by having a student-faculty committee cooperatively develop a code agreeable to all parties.

Hall Duty ("Guard Station No. 1 Reporting All's Well") Many teachers are assigned hall duty throughout the school day, even during lunch period or what in the profession is jokingly called

[3]Norma H. Compton, "Girls' Scholastic Achievement and Social Behavior," *Journal of Secondary Education* 42 (April, 1967): 166–168, reports the results of a study of 333 girls in physical education classes in three Utah high schools and 16 delinquent girls confined in the Utah State Industrial School. Using Pearson product moment correlation she found highly significant negative correlations resulted between appropriate dress and appearance scores and disciplinary action required. Girls with high appearance scores seldom required disciplinary action.

the teacher's free period. No one seriously believes that a hall will disappear, but some feel that students may wander around and get into trouble. So, the teacher is assigned to watch his section of the "front," challenging anyone who approaches with "Where's your hall pass?" usually followed by "Let me see it."

During the changing of classes, teachers are placed strategically to insure that students walk along the designated side of the corridor. In some schools students are even discouraged from getting a drink of water or visiting the rest rooms.

> "Move on, move on," Mr. Jones shouted as the students shuffled down the hall during the change of class. "Keep to your side of the white line! Stay away from that water fountain; there's no time for that now." After the hall was cleared, Mr. Jones paused at the door of the adjoining classroom and commented to his colleague, "Why don't we just let them run wild and kill each other?"

Is it really so terrible if students are allowed to move along the hall at their own pace (without a teacher prodding them), talking, jostling, maybe even laughing as they go from class to class. Some bruises might result; the noise level would rise; and there would be occasional traffic jams at the water fountains. Yet all this activity might release enough pent-up energy and tension to prevent disruptions in the classroom. But repressed students are going to be heard, even if they have to receive their knocks. By requiring his teachers to become wardens and to perform a nonprofessional function, the principal is influencing the rapport between a teacher and his students. As a result, some of the discipline problems occurring in the class may well have their origin in an encounter between teacher and student outside the classroom. Students will not believe that the teacher who yelled at them in the hall really cares about them once they enter the classroom. If assigned hall duty, teachers should exercise tact and treat students with the same respect and consideration they use in the classroom. Because he has been given an unpleasant task, the teacher should not vent his antagonism on students.

When Trouble Comes

Should a teacher feel he is unable to cope with a discipline problem he will expect assistance from the administration. There are principals who feel that anything which occurs within the classroom must be handled by the teacher himself.

Mr. Conklin was addressing the opening faculty meeting of the year. He closed with this statement, "One of the ways of evaluating a teacher's effectiveness is to count the number of students he sends to the office. Good teachers are able to handle their *own* problems."

Despite a teacher's intentions to deal with his own classroom problems, there are times when a student becomes so disruptive that he must be sent from the classroom. By sending a student to the office, the teacher is in effect asking for the principal's help. Immediately returning the student to the classroom without attempting to determine what triggered the student's action is no solution. In fact, it actually may intensify the student's problem. Since all behavior is caused, the principal, as a neutral party, may be able to work with the troubled student and the teacher to alleviate the pressures which resulted in a discipline problem.

Usually the principal is considered the court of last resort for classroom problems that teachers cannot solve themselves. In this role, the administrator is expected to mete out punishment for behavior that the teacher considers inappropriate and disruptive. Such a concept, however, is rather narrow and punitive in scope. The administrator should be viewed as an additional resource person, one who can assist the teacher in correcting problems rather than the individual whose only function is to punish those having problems.

Now Hear This

Another possible area of possible friction and disruption in the classroom can come through the overuse of the school's intercom system. Principals who habitually break in on a class period with, "I'm sorry to interrupt class but . . ." and then follow with some earth-shaking announcement like "all juniors must bring their money for the field trip tomorrow to the office by 3 p.m. today," has broken the chain of thought of every student and teacher in the school.

Of course, there are the morning and last period announcements that are *required listening*. Frequently the vital news is of such little consequence that the teacher himself does not listen. Yet he must attempt to keep the students quiet while word of the 10th-grade bake sale and the time of the golf team practice are intoned for one and all to hear.

Morning announcements are mercifully ended by the bell for the change of classes, but break-ins during a period can shatter the learning mood. If the flash comes during a test, it may work a very definite hardship on some students who find difficulty in regaining their train of thought. Announcements made at the end of the day are a signal that work is over—even if the teacher is in the middle of a sentence. When the magic box speaks, that's it for the day. Students who were actively involved in the lesson may become restless as they listen and seek diversion which can erupt into classroom disorder.

Many teachers and students resent the administrator who uses his public address system to quietly eavesdrop, making everyone feel that Big Brother is forever listening. Such a tactic could undermine the respect students have for their teachers since it might appear that the principal has little confidence in him and, therefore, feels it necessary to check on what he is doing.

This invasion of privacy may also make the teacher tense and likely to overreact to a minor classroom incident occurring when the intercom is on. The momentum will be lost, the mood broken, and both teacher and student angered. To circumvent this intrusion, the first person, teacher or student, hearing the click signifying that the intercom is on signals to the rest of the class. Then everyone remains quiet until a second click is heard, indicating the system has been turned off. A second action option would be for the teacher to invite the principal to visit his classroom personally to see the students in action.

Criticizing the Teacher

How will a student react to the public criticism of his teacher? This will depend in part on the teacher-student relationships that have been established in class. Yet the administrator who enters a teacher's classroom, interrupts his lesson, and then proceeds to berate him about some infraction of the rules in front of his students may precipitate problems for both teachers and students. In most cases, the teacher will become embarrassed and perhaps even defensive or angry. After the administrator has demonstrated his power and departed, the teacher may feel a need to reestablish his prestige and become oversensitive to the actions of his students and thus exercise his power on them. Unless students are more mature than their teacher, they too may retaliate against this expression of teacher power through deviant behavior. How has the teacher's image been affected? If the administrator's major function is to facilitate the teaching-learning process, how can such behavior by the principal help?

There are situations where the teacher will be found to be

totally wrong; in disputes, perhaps, involving students or parents. In such cases, a prudent administrator will give the teacher every opportunity to work the problem out himself, reserving any personal criticism for a private conference. For the same reason that teachers provide their students with every possible chance to save face in a tight situation, most principals realize that faculty members must hold the respect of both students and parents if they are to be effective in the classroom. Care should be taken not to diminish the teacher's prestige.

Administrators should also exercise caution when dealing directly with students. An adolescent who has been unduly or unjustly dealt with by the principal or a member of his staff may enter the classroom still licking his wounds. The severity of his offense and the disposition of the case will determine how he reacts to another authority figure, the teacher. He may be so up-tight that he explodes at an imagined teacher wrong. Even if he sits docilely through the period, how has his learning frame of reference been influenced? Since learning is the prime concern of the school, administrators should consider how their treatment of students either enhances or destroys this objective. The adolescent chewed out in the hall for a minor infraction of some rule will not enter his class with a mind set conducive to learning.

Assigning the Teacher to Classes

Principals always attempt to place teachers in their areas of specialization. But because of budgetary difficulties, increased enrollment problems, or a host of other reasons, this is not always possible. Since every class must have a teacher (even an unqualified teacher is better than no teacher, so the reasoning goes), a faculty member may find himself misassigned to a course completely out of his field. When this happens, he feels condemned to a lingering and frustrating existence.

Planning lessons in an unfamiliar subject (frequently one that is not the teacher's favorite) strains the limits of patience and perseverance. Learning new material well enough to teach it to others requires so much time that the teacher probably will be forced to neglect classes in his specialty. This only heightens his sense of frustration (and students are quick to spot a "frustrated" teacher). Under such circumstances, it is extremely difficult, if not impossible, for the teacher to be enthusiastic, relaxed, or confident. Without these attributes the class will become tense and the likelihood of discipline problems developing will increase.

Administrators know that a potentially explosive situation

exists when a teacher has been misassigned. Yet the necessity of placing a teacher in a classroom is considered to outweigh any disadvantages to both teacher and students. This reasoning is understandable from an administrative point of view.

Before accepting any teaching assignment, a teacher should determine if he can do justice to the students taking the course. Any teacher who is just marking time until a competent replacement can be found will be unable to guide the learning activities of the class in a positive direction. Should discipline problems develop because of frustration and boredom, who is to blame? The student? The administrator? The teacher?

Summary

Amidst critics, the school principal must focus on effective administration of the school to provide quality education for all his students. In charting his operational procedures, he sometimes assigns teachers additional duties that, because they are of a disciplinary or regulatory nature, could conflict with their teaching roles.

When a teacher finds himself with a classroom situation he is unable to handle, he expects his principal to help with whatever assistance and support are necessary.

Frustrations and repercussions can result from criticizing teachers publicly and misassigning them.

We have attempted to identify some of the difficulties faced by today's secondary school administrator and to indicate how the interpretation and execution of his duties can reduce or intensify the classroom discipline problems his teachers encounter.

Situations Caused by Administrators

The following pages present situations in which discipline was affected by some action of the school administrator.

Situation 1: Where There's Smoke There's Cigarettes. Mr. Atkins was following an administrative request that teachers periodically check rest rooms near their classes for students smoking when he entered the boys' room on the third floor. The air was heavy with smoke. Chip Williams was standing innocently beside a ground-out butt.

It was obvious that Chip had a lung full of smoke and didn't know how to get rid of it without Mr. Atkins seeing him. His face was turning red as Mr. Atkins waited, knowing that Chip *had* to exhale eventually. Finally, a burst of smoke shot from Chip's mouth. Before Mr. Atkins could say anything, Chip snapped his fingers, "Damn it's *cold* in here," and started for the door. Mr. Atkins . . .

Action Options

1. . . . called him back for a visit to the principal's office.

2. . . . warned Chip that smoking was against the rules but that he would give him another chance.

3. . . . laughed at his quick thinking and said nothing.

4. ... told him it was at least 85 degrees in the room and *that* was cigarette smoke.

5. ... (your solution)

Situation 2: Can You Prove It?   Mrs. Olson entered the principal's office. "I caught Freddy Jackson cheating on his final exam."

"How do you know he was cheating?" inquired the principal.

"Look," Mrs. Olson said, "He was copying the answers from *this* piece of paper. What should I do?"

The principal looked at the paper. "Are *all* the answers to your exam on this sheet?"

"No, of course not. No one knew exactly what questions would be on the final."

"Then how can you accuse him of cheating? Did you ask Freddy if he was cheating?"

"No, but I saw him with this sheet of paper," stated Mrs. Olson.

The principal shook his head, "I'm sorry but this evidence is not sufficient."

At this point, Mrs. Olson realized . . .

Action Options

1. . . . her principal was not going to support her and punish the student for cheating so she had better drop the entire matter.

2. . . . since her principal was not going to support her, she would have to take matters into her own hands and fail the student.

3. . . . that she really didn't have sufficient evidence and
    apologized for bothering the principal.

4. . . . that perhaps she should talk with Freddy before
    taking any further action.

5. . . . (your solution)

Situation 3: The Absent-Minded Teacher.   Mr. Edward's industrial arts class was noisily occupied with various projects when the principal marched into the room, obviously very angry. "Mr. Edwards, do you realize that it is now 8:30? Do you know what that means?"

"No, not really," Mr. Edwards responded blankly.

"Well then, I'll tell you what it means. It means that Mrs. Patterson, the attendance secretary, has been sitting at her typewriter for the past 20 minutes waiting for your absentee list. The entire school's absentee report cannot be typed because you did not consider it important enough to send your list in on time."

"Oh! Well, . . ." began Mr. Edwards.

"You'd better have a good reason, Edwards. This kind of thing cannot be tolerated. I'm waiting."

Since Mr. Edwards could sense that his entire class was also waiting, he . . .

Action Options
1. . . . apologized and said that it wouldn't happen again.

2. . . . told him that his class had become so involved he completely forgot about the list.

3. . . . became angry and told the principal never to come into his class like that again.

4. . . . offered to discuss the matter during his planning period and then made out the list and gave it to the principal.

5. . . . (your solution)

Suggested Readings

Ackerly, Robert. *The Reasonable Exercise of Authority.* Washington, D.C.: National Association of Secondary School Principals, 1969. Briefly presents the concept of due process, citing a position on ten issues concerning student rights.

Cutts, Norma E., and Moseley, Nicholas. *Teaching The Disorderly Pupil in Elementary and Secondary School*. New York: Longman's, Green and Co., 1959. Chap. 2. Discusses the administration and the teacher's approach to discipline.

Fish, Kenneth L. *Conflict and Dissent in the High School*. New York: Bruce Books, 1970. Emphasizes racial tension in schools and describes the role of the teacher in coping with schoolwide disorders.

Jessup, Michael H. *"OATS* Program for Beginning Teachers." *School and Community* 56, No. 14 (December, 1969) : 30, 32–33. This article develops the importance of orientation, assignment, time, and success in the professional growth of beginning teachers.

Ovard, Glen F. *Administration of the Changing Secondary School*. New York: The Macmillan Company, 1966. Chap. 13. Discussion of how administrators can help teachers effectively reduce their discipline problems. Administrative methods of dealing with student problems are presented.

5

Parent-Caused Problems

The final co-stars in that great American production of getting-an-education are the parents. To illustrate their importance, just ask yourself, "What would our schools be without parents?" Empty. Admittedly, therefore, parents are necessary. So, let us look at today's parents. Who are they? How do they influence the classroom behavior of their children?

Today's adult is better educated than his parents or the parents of any previous generation.[1] His achievements range from winning the most cataclysmic war in the history of the world to putting a man on the moon. The standard of living he enjoys is the highest ever and constantly improving. Despite such progress, these accomplishments have not brought peace and contentment. Instead, we find him anxious over the state of the world, troubled by racial discord, poverty, and the future of the economy. Man, with all his power and knowledge, finds himself struggling to live in harmony with his fellow man on a planet threatened by war and pollution.

Perhaps his greatest source of frustration is, at the

[1]Cyril O. Houle, "Goals for 1970," *Adult Leadership* 10 (May, 1961): 2.

same time, the source of his greatest pride—his children. They are his own flesh and blood and naturally he wants the best for them. So, although many would find it difficult to verbalize exactly what they want for their children beyond happiness, parental expectations are high. Some dream of the college education which they missed or a job in the skilled trades for their children. At times, parents are, without thinking, attempting to recapture their youth or ambitions through the lives of others. The child's interests and capabilities are ignored. If parental goals are unrealistic in terms of their son's or daughter's ability, tremendous pressures descend upon the teenager as he struggles to meet these expectations.

As the child matures, pressures continue to build. Parents may suddenly discover that communication between them and their children has been severely impaired, if not completely severed. To further complicate the situation, a little of their pride disappears with the realization that their children, who just a short time ago revered them as the source of all knowledge, now may cast them in the role of the village idiot. Advice or suggestions are greeted with pained expressions and comments like, "Oh, Dad, you just don't understand. It's not the same as when *you* were young." (Dad receives the distinct impression that his child believes he was a classmate of George Washington.)

Yet, what these adolescents say is true. The world is not the same as it was when their fathers and mothers were growing up (a problem common to every generation). Failure to understand and accept these changes is a major cause of friction between the generations.

Adolescent values and ambitions for the future are no longer inherited from their parents and accepted without question. Going into the family business, making more money than dear ol' Dad, or marrying the right person are not considered as essential for the good life by many. The overriding concern of most adolescents is their search for self-identity. Parents play a decisive role in this search for self.[2] Their influence as models for the child can never be dismissed as insignificant.

Mrs. Jennings had sent a note home with Peggy requesting a parent conference. Peggy's standardized tests indicated she had above average intelligence, but her grades were bordering on failure. Of equal importance

[2]For a discussion of the adolescent's development see Karl C. Garrison, *Psychology of Adolescence*, 6th ed. (Englewood Cliffs, N.J.: Prentice-Hall, Inc., 1965).

was her attitude. She was hostile toward everyone in the class.

The following day, when asked if her parents had responded to the note, Peggy replied, "My father said he's too busy and a conference would be a waste of time. There is nothing wrong with my attitude. He never did good in school but he has lots of money and can buy and sell any teacher. That's what's important."

The home environment of the teenagers in any one class could be as varied as the number of students. Teachers often forget that the emotional climate under which the adolescent exists will, to a large extent, influence his school behavior. Therefore, the way in which the parent perceives education is important since the adolescent may reflect these views.

Most parents are concerned about education. The parent who seeks to be actively involved in his child's education now sees his role changing from the unseen hand dutifully signing report cards, ready to discipline at a word from the principal, to an individual conversant with the school's philosophy, curriculum, and staff.

Unfortunately, the majority of parents are uninvolved. School is school's business. Usually, contact only occurs when trouble develops and the pleasure of their company is requested by a teacher or administrator. Perhaps remembering unhappy experiences when they were students, some parents are extremely reluctant to set foot in school.

Becoming a parent does not automatically bestow all the wisdom needed for the part, and many parents feel themselves poorly equipped to fulfill their responsibilities. Often as the child reaches adolescence and asserts his independence, some parents, feeling threatened and less sure of themselves, may demand blind obedience to their whims and wishes. They are afraid to let go and admit that their child is growing up. Thus, the adolescent is placed in a precarious state. He wants to obey and please his parents. Yet, at the same time, he is striving to discover his own worth as an individual. How can this be accomplished if those who are closest to him do not believe his contributions are of value?

A frequent complaint of teenagers about their parents is that they do not listen to them. Now listening does not mean agreeing to every statement, every demand, and teenagers will admit this (though maybe with grudging reluctance). But they want to be heard and their words considered important by adults close to them. When an adolescent is ignored at home, he may seek his identity in the classroom through aggressive behavior that commands the attention of his teacher and peers.

The Big Cover-Up

Parents who permit their teenagers habitually to remain home from school or cover up for them when they skip school are doing their children a disservice. They may realize that for some reason they do not like school and believe they are helping them by not forcing them to go. Nothing could be further from the truth. If school is the problem, remaining away from school is not the solution.

A student who consistently avoids school probably does so because he is unable to find success in the classroom. Rather than feel the constant humiliation and frustration of failure, the adolescent seeks escape through some form of nonschool activity. But this only works for as long as he remains away from school. Once he returns to class, he must face a more intense situation than he left. Additional work has been covered; he is further behind; the alienation has deepened.

We mentioned earlier in the book how to bring the student back into the mainstream of class activity. For this procedure to be successful, however, the student must want help. If he is too far behind, he may feel it is hopeless and give up. Here is where the teacher may need the cooperation of the parents if he is to reach the student. Pressure (the concept of failure) must be removed while the student catches up. Until the student feels that he can function as a member of the class, he will remain a mental drop-out, a potential physical drop-out, and a probable disciplinary problem.

Often teachers believe they know the reason why a student is out of school and they react negatively when the child returns, even if he has an approved note. If he missed an exam, there are teachers who would fix him by giving a make-up test guaranteed to stump a Ph.D. Or they may place unreasonable demands upon him to complete the assignments. Attitudes such as these only intensify the student's problem.

> Tim averaged two absences each week. He always had a note the next day, signed by his mother (his father was dead), stating that he had been ill.
> His math teacher, Mr. Mackey, tried repeatedly to talk with Tim but the youth claimed nothing was wrong. Phone calls to his mother brought no results. Tim fell far-

ther behind in his work until he was barely passing. One day when Tim was absent, Mr. Mackey saw the visiting teacher and asked her to stop by his student's house.

The reason for the absences became clear. Tim's mother was an alcoholic. When she was ill, he stayed home to care for her. Other times, Tim would remain home to clean up the mess his mother had made of the house the previous night.

When a student is consistently missing school and his absences are being sanctioned by a parent, the teacher must consider two sets of motives: the student's and the parent's. The student may be following the wishes of his parents and not want to expose their reasons to outsiders. Hence, he may appear to be uninterested in school. Until the teacher gains insight into the full situation, he will have difficulty working with the student.

Keeping Junior in Line

When the adolescent gets himself (or herself) into enough trouble—academic or behavioral—the administration usually requests a parent conference. Depending upon the parent's attitude (how he interprets his reason for being at the meeting) the visit may range from confrontation to cooperation.

The military officer, or his civilian prototype, who storms the principal's office as if it were Normandy Beach to discuss his son's misbehavior may be expressing his own feelings of inadequacy when he states the school does not know how to handle the situation. According to him, the teachers are incapable of leadership. They coddle the troops too much. If he were in charge, there would be no nonsense. Should the teacher concerned with the misbehavior suggest that the father might share some of his disciplinary know-how with son, Bill, he is likely to be told that making Bill behave in school is the school's business, not his.

Some fathers, feeling they have failed in providing the proper behavioral model for their youngster and reluctant to admit this, may use a bluff and bluster approach to hide a feeling of despair. "Go ahead and smack him in the mouth if he gets out of line or gives you any lip. You have my permission."

Perhaps this is part of the problem. The parent does smack him in the mouth whenever he attempts to express himself. As a result, the student uses the classroom as a forum for his ideas, disrupting the learning activities in the process. Or, just the opposite could be true. In some homes, there is very little parental guidance. The adolescent is forced to make his own decisions and then live by the outcome. It is little wonder that, in his search for direction, he may select the wrong path.

As the teacher looks for the causes of a student's behavioral problem, the attitudes of the parents toward school, learning, and teachers (in particular) must be given strong consideration. Good teachers quickly learn to recognize the overly strict and the too permissive parent. Of equal concern to teachers is the parent who constantly pressures his child to excel beyond the limits of his capabilities. The adolescent driven by his parents to make good grades, be in the top section of the accelerated program, or play first string on the varsity football team, may become a discipline problem, hoping secretly to be bounced from class and thus reduce some of the pressure. Or a student who feels he cannot meet his parents' expectations may simply withdraw and refuse to even try.

Who is the Student?

When it comes to the student's academic program, parents may cause difficulty for both their child and his teacher. As we have mentioned before, if parental expectations and their child's ability and interests are at variance, the student may reflect his frustration in his classroom behavior.

For example, after school begins Carol's mother wants Carol put in Algebra I immediately ("Of course she is going to college even if she said she wanted to go to beauty school after she graduates. After all, she's only fourteen. What does she know?") Reminding Carol's mother that her daughter's math ability is nil probably will accomplish nothing. Carol has told her mother, math teacher, and counselor that she positively, absolutely, and finally does not want to take algebra. Yet, by the next day there is a strong possibility that Carol will be sitting in an Algebra I class. When this happens, the problem for the entire school year may well be "Who will suffer more, Carol or her math teacher?"

If the school is unable to convince a parent that his child's abilities and interest lie in a different area, the student may find himself consigned to an academic schedule in which he can find little meaning. As the days slowly pass and his frustrations mount, his hostility may become open. Since the teacher will see only the release of this hostility, he may not consider the real cause of the problem.

Some parents resist programs which they feel are nonacademic or special reasoning that their child will be stigmatized as second rate. Feelings such as this are difficult for the teacher to handle. The parent's ego is at stake, and he may forget that his child's ability should determine his type of studies. It will require a considerable degree of tact for the teacher to convince the parent that the growth and success of his child are at stake.

The Mark of Success

Perhaps the most vexing problem and one very likely to bring the parent to school is the matter of that *B*, or *C*, or *D*, or *F* on the report card. (There have been no recorded instances where a parent complained about an *A* or reported the grade to be an error requesting that it be lowered.) Why do some parents become so upset about grades? How do their reactions affect the classroom behavior of their offspring?

There are probably three major reasons why parents become so disturbed about grades. First, grades are subjective. Junior high school boys often discover teacher bias as women tend to grade them lower than the girls in class. Boys may not measure up to a male teacher's expectations. A physical education teacher told one of the authors that he couldn't stand boys who came to school with their hair combed and shoes shined. (The implication was that if a boy was neat, he wasn't much of a boy.) Parents realize that teachers are not always objective in their evaluation procedures. Therefore, should their child believe that his grade was not representative of his work, parental intervention could be forthcoming.

Second, parents believe their child deserves a higher grade because . . . (Here are some of the choices usually offered:)

> "Why, Mary goes up to her room right after dinner and studies until she goes to bed, so how could she get anything less than an *A*?" (The fact that Mary's hi-fi is blaring the entire time plus the nine nightly telephone calls may go unnoticed by the parent.)

> "My John has always gotten *A*s." (Implying that any teacher who would not follow in the great established tradition is either stupid, misguided, or un-American.)

> "Mary said the reason you gave her a *C* is that you don't like her. You give the people you like *A*s and *B*s." (Likeable Mary has not mentioned to mama that she has

yet to turn in one homework assignment for the entire quarter.)

"Charles tries; it's not his fault he hasn't any mathematical ability. His father wasn't too good in math either." (After all, you can't fight heredity.)

"If Jane doesn't get an *A* in English, she won't be accepted at Exclusive U. And if she doesn't get accepted there, I can't think what she might do." (Do you want her suicide on your conscience?)

Third, and perhaps the heart of the problem, parents may see the grade as a statement of their own ability or intelligence. If their child does not succeed, they may consider it to be a reflection upon themselves.

The student of overachieving parents who brings home a report card bearing anything but *A*s and *B*s may receive a cool reception from his parents. A *C* indicates average performance and no one wants to be average. (It is strange that we claim to be a nation of "average Americans," yet few want to be the parents of an average or below average child.) The majority of the human race are average in the majority of things they undertake. This is what average is all about. Everyone has special talents, things in which he excels. But almost everyone also will display weakness in other areas and thus be considered average or below average in those fields. Consequently it is simply asking the impossible to demand that a student excel across the board. But year after year some parents maintain constant pressure for good grades in every course and *C* is not considered good. Is it any wonder that more and more students dislike school?

Parents could help their teenagers tremendously if they would develop the proper perspective on grades. If they know their son is putting forth his best effort and still does not receive more than a *C* (average), accepting the grade which he earned and praising him for his work is the most sensible, practical, and humane reaction. The adolescent can then concentrate on learning instead of grades, knowing his parents are not expecting miracles in subjects in which he has little aptitude.

Teachers can help reduce parental pressure for grades by stressing the value of learning for self-betterment (not for getting a higher grade), and by measuring (grading) students in terms of their individual growth (not in comparison to others in the class). Only then will discipline problems resulting from our present concept of school success be eliminated.

Summary

In this chapter, we focused on parents and some of the ways they can affect the classroom behavior of their children. The adolescent's home environment will play a major part in how he acts in school. If the student is unable to withstand the various pressures exerted by his parents to take certain courses, make certain grades, he may find his release in the classroom through deviant behavior.

Situations Caused by Parents

The following pages present actual situations in which discipline was affected by some action of a parent.

Situation 1: Student Ability   Donna Clark was waiting for Mr. Miller when he arrived for his first period U.S. history class. "My mother was upset about that *F* you gave me," she told him.

"She should be, Donna. You didn't do *any* work during the entire term. As I have told you many times, if you would stop causing trouble in class and pay attention, you would be able to pass. But you don't even try!"

"Well," said Donna, holding out a folded piece of paper, "mother said to give you this."

Mr. Miller read the note: "Donna is stupid. How can you fail a person who can't do the work. It won't do any good."

"Donna, did you read this?" he asked.

"Yes."

"Do you believe you're stupid?"

"Yes."

Mr. Miller looked first at the note and then at Donna. She was slow, but she certainly was not stupid. Since he knew that Donna could do passing work if she wanted to, he . . .

Action Options

1. . . . told her if she would behave in class and try to do the work he would pass her.

2. . . . thanked Donna for the note and after class phoned her mother and asked her to please come in and talk with him about her daughter's ability.

3. ... told Donna to shape up and get to work. He was not going to pass any loafers.

4. ... later asked the guidance counselor to arrange a conference with Donna *and* her mother to clarify the misconceptions about Donna's ability to experience success in school.

5. ... (your solution)

Situation 2: Let's All Go To The Ball Game   It was the opening day of the World Series. Not surprisingly, absentee rate at Babe Ruth High reflected the event. So, in homeroom the next day, when Jim, Don, Ray, and Jack (called the Four Musketeers because they always were seen together) approached Mr. Baker's desk, he smiled and said, "Well, boys, did you enjoy the game yesterday?" They started to laugh and all but Jack readily admitted that they had gone to the game and so didn't have a note from home. Mr. Baker began writing unexcused absence slips for each when Jack silently placed a note on his desk. Mr. Baker read it. "Jack, do you mean to stand there and tell me you didn't go to that game yesterday with your friends?"

Jack looked sheepish, "What does the note say, Mr. Baker? Doesn't it say I was home, sick?"

The other three boys looked at Jack strangely but didn't say a word. Mr. Baker should . . .

Action Options
1. . . . accept the note as written, giving Jack an excused absence.

2. . . . refuse to accept the note, telling Jack that he knows he went to the game.

3. . . . tell Jack he doesn't believe him and insist his parents come to school to discuss the matter.

4. . . . question the other boys, hoping they will implicate Jack.

5. . . . (your solution)

Situation 3: Belated Interest   Entering the room, Mr. Connor knew that it was going to be quite a parent-teacher conference. The school term would end in one month and Jerry Thompson was failing senior English. Besides constantly being sarcastic in class, what work he had turned in during the year had proven to be someone else's or of failing quality. Despite several requests for a conference, Mr. Thompson had refused to discuss Jerry's behavior or lack of performance. Then, after notices were sent to the parents of those students who would not graduate, he immediately requested a conference to determine if "anything could be done."

Since he anticipated a stormy session based on previous discussions with Mr. Thompson over the telephone, Mr. Connor had requested that Mrs. Stanley, the senior guidance counselor, be present. Jerry was also there at the request of his father.

Mr. Thompson suggested extra-credit work be used to offset Jerry's previous failures. This was vetoed by Mr. Connor. "A complete term's work cannot be covered with a few papers. Besides, as I told you, Jerry's mother admitted that *she* wrote his last several papers."

Mr. Thompson started to reply when Jerry interrupted. "Dammit, Dad, shut up. Can't you see talking to him's a waste of time. He's gonna fail me."

Mr. Connor . . .

Action Options

1. . . . suggested that perhaps Mrs. Stanley should explain to Mr. Thompson some of the problems which the staff had encountered with Jerry during the year.

2. . . . asked Mrs. Stanley to assure Jerry that they were only interested in his future growth.

3. ... informed Mr. Thompson that Jerry's outburst and lack of respect were typical of his overall school performance.

4. ... terminated the conference stating that Jerry had failed and further discussion was pointless.

5. ... asked Jerry how he felt that he could possibly pass the course.

6. ... (your solution)

Suggested Readings

Dreikurs, Rudolf. *Psychology in the Classroom*. 2d ed. New York: Harper & Row, Publishers, 1968. Chap. 2. The influence of the family on the development of the child.

Grambs, Jean Dresden. *Schools, Scholars, and Society*. Englewood Cliffs, N.J.: Prentice-Hall, Inc., 1965. Chap. 6. An examination of rural, suburban, and urban community structures and the effects of each on students.

Henderson, George, and Bibens, Robert F. *Teachers Should Care: Social Perspectives of Teaching*. New York: Harper & Row, Publishers, 1970. Chap. 5. A positive look at parents, their concerns about education, and how they can help the teacher.

Perel, William M., and Vairo, Philip D. *Urban Education: Problems and Prospects*. New York: David McKay Company, Inc., 1969. Chap. 2. A discussion of the cultural backgrounds of urban students in relationship to the school curriculum.

Reichart, Stanford. *Change and the Teacher: The Philosophy of A Social Phenomenon*. New York: Thomas Y. Crowell Co., 1969. Chap. 3. Various pressures which parents exert on the teacher.

Thomas, R. Murray. *Aiding the Maladjusted Pupil: A Guide for Teachers*. New York: David McKay Company, Inc., 1967. Chap. 4. A discussion of the various ways in which the student's environment can be changed to aid his adjustment.

6

Conclusions

In the preceding five chapters, we have examined, scrutinized, and reflected upon the various types of discipline problems which could befall the teacher, problems caused by students, parents, administrators, even by the teacher himself. Now, finally, what conclusions can be drawn?

The fainthearted might reply that teaching is definitely not for them. The cynic might say that no one could accomplish teaching and taming simultaneously. Yet obviously thousands of teachers are extremely successful in both endeavors. Not only are they successful, they also enjoy what they are doing. The few discipline problems encountered do not defeat or discourage them —which leads us to the first of our conclusions:

1. MANY INCONSEQUENTIAL INCIDENTS WHICH BECOME FULL-BLOWN CRISES COULD HAVE BEEN CONTROLLED.

The inexperienced, immature, or insensitive teacher often precipitates problems in his own classroom by permitting little situations to be magnified out of proportion. The teacher who feels no responsibility for developing self-discipline on the part of his student will attempt to rule unilaterally (a course guaranteed to cause problems). Adolescents, probing to find out "Who am I?" also ask "Why should I?" when a teacher arbitrarily attempts to impose his authority. Thus the teacher who makes no effort to aid students in recognizing the need for self-discipline may find himself locked in a bitter struggle for control of the class. Even the teacher who finds himself in difficulty through no fault of his own can minimize and contain situations. Through the judicious selection of the appropriate action option, the proper degree of understanding, and just the right amount of good humor, he can prevent an incident from being a crisis.

Empathy with his students and an awareness of their moods will enable the teacher to adapt lessons and pace activities in order to avoid any serious disruptions to the learning process while providing an atmosphere most conducive to learning and self-growth.

After dissecting the personality, pressures, and need of today's adolescents in Chapter Three, a second conclusion seems justified.

2. ADOLESCENTS EXPECT AND WILL ACCEPT BEHAVIORAL LIMITS IN AN ATMOSPHERE CONDUCIVE TO SELF-GROWTH AND LEARNING.

As teeenagers move through the stages from adolescent to adult, their search for self-identity intensifies. The teacher must accept each student as a unique personality, an individual of worth, deserving respect and acceptance. He must also realize that, as a teacher and as an adult, he should represent a model of mature, responsible, and consistent behavior for his students. (Today's teenagers have enough pals in their own age bracket; they neither need nor wish teachers to be numbered in this group.)

The emotional climate in the classroom should be such that a student is encouraged to voice opinions, question statements, and arrive at his own conclusions. His contributions in class should be encouraged, for through participation and group interaction, he will better understand his own beliefs and feelings as well as those of others. Thus he will develop a greater empathy for those around him and, consequently, a sharper awareness of the problems which face him.

Secondary school students realize they have responsibilities to their teachers, peers, parents, and to themselves. If the proper class atmosphere is provided by the teacher, free from sarcasm, fear, or ridicule, students will accept their role as part of an educational community. As contributing members, they understandably desire some voice in determining how they shall be governed. Shared responsibility then becomes the key to cooperation—and coexistence—in the classroom.

Yet regardless of how fairly the teacher treats his students, that fateful day will come when trouble finds its way into the classroom. Though it may seem an obvious truism, we have found that some teachers, even the experienced, seem to forget our third conclusion.

3. SINCE ALL BEHAVIORAL PROBLEMS ARE CAUSED, THE TEACHER MUST BECOME A DIAGNOSTICIAN.

Much of the time teaching is comparatively smooth sailing. When trouble does occur in the classroom, it may not be possible to ascertain the cause immediately. The teacher's grasp of his subject matter may be superior and his teaching strategies appropriate and effective. The student may have had no intention of precipitating a crisis. Then something happens. Invariably the cause of the difficulty is a breakdown in communications, a misunderstanding of a verbal or nonverbal signal by one or both parties. Once trouble develops, it is the handling and disposition of the situation that separates the men from the boys, the professionals from the hacks.

The insecure teacher, hiding feelings of professional or personal inadequacy, may lack the courage to enlist the aid of the administration or the parents in seeking the cause of behavioral or academic problems that he is unable to solve. The professional teacher does not hesitate to involve anyone necessary to discover a solution. His ability to reconcile the many, complex interrelationships between students, parents, and the administration reduces discipline problems. This fact leads inevitably to the conclusion that

4. AN EFFECTIVE TEACHER WILL HAVE FEWER PROBLEMS, ACADEMIC AND BEHAVIORAL, IN HIS CLASSROOM BECAUSE OF HIS PROFESSIONAL COMPETENCE AND PERSONAL QUALITIES.

As the title implies, the effective teacher has a command of the subject matter. He has organized and planned material and developed teaching strategies to communicate this specialized knowledge with an effectiveness that provides real meaning to his students. He recognizes that the selection of the material taught and the teaching techniques employed are contingent upon the ability and interest levels of his students. Course goals were cooperatively determined by teacher and students at the beginning of the school year. Thus, by attempting to involve students in the work of the class, the effective teacher will have fewer and less serious discipline problems. Here, then, is the creative combination of knowing *what* to teach and *how* to teach.

The effective teacher is also confident, experiencing success in a profession he finds satisfying and rewarding. A sense of mutual respect characterizes his relations with students, colleagues, parents, and administration. Since his own self-image is secure and well-defined, he does not interpret minor incidents as personally directed or threatening. As a mature adult, able to recognize his strengths and accept his shortcomings, he can empathize with his students and maintain an appropriate emotional climate in the classroom.

His confidence stems not only from his own personality, but also from his academic competence and knowledge of adolescent psychology and the principles of learning. He recognizes the necessity for continued learning in his discipline—that every good teacher is always a learner. If his teaching is to be effective, the unique characteristics of the adolescent must be understood and then reflected in the teaching procedures utilized. Their individual needs and developmental patterns must also be recognized. Understanding theories of learning aids in developing appropriate teaching methods and devising techniques to ignite student motivation and reduce discipline problems.

Yet beyond psychology and subject matter lies the area of acceptance, of mutual respect between teacher and pupils. The effective teacher likes his students. Though it is not possible to like every student equally (and some teenagers seemingly defy anyone to like them), the successful teacher conveys his intent to like each and every one.

Enthusiasm for his subject is another characteristic of the effective teacher. Teaching is often an exhausting business and requires massive doses of energy to survive the endless rounds of classes, conferences, meetings, lesson planning, paper grading, and so forth. Those who dislike teaching a particular subject or who feel uncomfortable in the classroom will be unwilling to expend that energy. The enthusiastic teacher transmits a sense of vitality about his subject to students, who find themselves engulfed by the momentum he generates in the lesson. Any teacher who does not believe his field has relevance in today's world will never convince a skeptical adolescent.

Another ingredient for reducing behavioral problems in the classroom is teacher empathy. Understanding the problems of teenagers is often not enough. The teacher should attempt to see the world through the eyes of the adolescent, thus giving him greater perception and insight into their lives. Though a certain degree of objectivity must be maintained, sensitivity to troubled adolescents can strengthen rapport between teacher and students and further reduce the possibility of discipline problems.

Yet some teachers honestly feel that the personal and academic concerns of students can—and should—be totally separated. Nothing is further from the truth. A student worried about a personal problem will find it difficult to concentrate on learning and his behavior may become disruptive. The empathetic teacher recognizes this and does not overreact. Students, acutely aware of the atmosphere in the classroom, should respond favorably to the adult concerned about them not only as learners but as unique individuals—as human beings.

Chapters Four and Five explored how forces outside the classroom, administrators and parents, could affect classroom discipline. Summing up our findings, we conclude that

5. THE TEACHER DOES NOT OPERATE IN A VACUUM NOR RESTRICT HIS ACTIVITIES TO HIS CLASSROOM—TOTAL INVOLVEMENT IS ESSENTIAL TO SUCCESSFUL DISCIPLINE.

If a teacher is to achieve maximum effectiveness, he must become involved and aware of what is going on around him. Those who believe that a student's education begins and ends within the four walls of their classrooms do themselves and their students an injustice and pave the way for possible disciplinary situations. Lines of communication between teachers, administrators, and parents must be kept open and viable so that student interests, concerns, and problems can be easily identified and readily discussed before a crisis situation develops.

Summary

As we look back on our conclusions, it becomes evident that the majority of problems which develop in the classroom stem from poor interpersonal relations with students, colleagues, the administration, or parents. The suggestions we have made to ease some of the tensions and eliminate some of the strife are the result of experience. The techniques discussed have proven successful when used in secondary schools. They work. So why not go ahead, try them, and see for yourself? What can you lose?

Index